101 Baby Travel Tips

LifeTips Book Series

By Christina Chan
Baby Travel Guru
LifeTips

LifeTips Book Series
Boston, Massachusetts

Text copyright © 2006 LifeTips. All rights reserved.

LIFETIPS PRESIDENT: Byron White

BOOK SERIES EDITOR: Melanie Nayer

All rights reserved. No part of this book may be reproduced in any form, by photostat, microfilm, xerography, or any other means, or incorporated into any information retrieval system, electronic or mechanical, without the written permission of the copyright owner. All inquires should be addressed to:

LifeTips.com, Inc.

101 Book Series

One First Avenue

Building 34, Suite 200

Charlestown, MA 02129

(617) 886-9001

http://www.LifeTips.com

International Standard Book No. 978-1-60275-007-4

This book is intended for use as an informational guide and entertainment purposes and should not be used as a substitute for any professional medical care or treatment, professional legal advice or professional financial guidance.

Table of Contents

A Note from the Editor	4
A Note from the Author	5
Air Travel with Babies	7
Baby Car Seats	17
Baby Carriers	25
Baby Friendly Vacations	33
Baby Strollers	55
Baby Travel Accessories	67
Baby Travel Gear For Meals	73
Baby Travel Gear for Sleeping	81
Baby Travel Safety	89
Baby Travel Toys	107
Cruise Travel with Babies	119
Outdoor Travel with Babies	129
Road Trips with Baby	139

A Note from the Editor

We all love to travel. Whether it's to an exotic location via cruise ship, or a secluded cabin in the mountains, there is a vacation for everyone. But what do you do with baby? Thanks to these tips, it's even easier to bring baby along for the ride!

Christina Chan has taken her years of expertise - and motherhood - and crafted these tips for travel-hungry families who are eager to hit the road with baby, without all the fuss. From disposal bottles to passport regulations, Christina hits all the important aspects of the travel planning process to ensure a smooth trip.

Not sure where to go? No problem! Take a look at Christina's favorite family-friendly destinations and get tips on saving a few bucks, too. And make sure to read the not-so-family friendly vacation spots, too.

Thanks to her interviews with baby experts and extraordinary moms, Christina has created 101 tips that are sure to bring your family fun, and ease, with baby on your next vacation outing.

Happy Travels!

Melanie Nayer
Editor, LifeTips.com

A Note from the Author

Just because you have an infant doesn't mean you have to put your travel plans on hold. Traveling with an infant can be a daunting task. But we're here to make it not only doable - but fun. Whether you're a seasoned parent or just expecting, 101 Baby Travel Tips offers something for everyone who wants to get away from it all with baby. Here are just some of the highlights you can expect:

• Planning a cruise? Find out which cruise lines have what amenities just for parents and babies.

• Think you'll have to rule out a tropical escape? You can go and bring baby. Find out where.

• Not sure what to pack for the plane? We'll tell you what essentials you need to consider.

• Wondering what some of the latest baby travel gear products are? We'll fill you in on our favorite finds.

• Are some hotels better for bringing your infant? There are and we'll tell you which ones.

• Dreading that road trip with baby? Find out how you can stay sane.

• Worried about health hazards abroad? We'll tell you how to keep healthy and how to prepare for an emergency.

Come along for the ride and let these tips help you create a well-planned, safe, and fun travel experience for you and your baby.

Christina Chan
LifeTips Expert Guru

Air Travel with Babies

1| Take-off On Our Ear Opening Advice

Have you ever been on a flight and while the plane is descending, you hear the blood-curdling scream of an infant two rows behind you? It may have been due to air pressure in the ears, which affects infant ears much more than it does adult ears. According to Yahoo pediatric expert Dr. Green, the landing is always harder on infant ears than take-off. This is because during take-off the ears tend to adjust spontaneously. However, during landing, the rising pressure can cause pain and the adjustment doesn't occur spontaneously, but requires the motions of yawning, swallowing, or crying. Rather than letting your infant work out the air pressure changes alone, you can alleviate the problem.

- If you're nursing your infant, do so during take-off. The swallowing action naturally helps remove the pressure in baby's ears and with any luck your child might fall asleep. If your infant can wait, don't nurse during taxiing. Instead, see if you can nurse when the plane is almost ready to lift off the ground.

- If you're bottle-feeding, do so during take-off. Pacifiers can also work as well. For toddlers, chewing on munchies and drinking out of a sippy cup will help. Though most toddlers are well past the stage of painful ear pressure due to plane travel.

2| Baby Carrier or Stroller?

You have two main accessories for getting baby through the airport - a baby carrier or the stroller. Which one is better? Well, that depends. Baby carriers do offer advantages. You can dodge crowds much easier, your hands will be free, you won't have a bulky piece of equipment to lug around, and it's calming for infants and young toddlers to be held close to you. However, you'll also have to bear the weight of carrying your child through the airport (which might be minimal if you choose the right carrier) and you won't have the benefit of having your stroller at your destination.

Baby Bjorn is a popular front carrier for many parents. If this is your pick, we recommend you get the model with the lumbar support for your comfort. *Ergo* makes a comfortable soft carrier, excellent for back carries and toddlers.

Strollers make it a little more difficult to navigate, but you won't have to worry about handling the extra weight; at least until your infant or toddler wants to be picked up. You'll also have something to wheel your little one around in when you get to your destination. If you decide to go the stroller route, one way to keep things to a minimum is with a lightweight stroller or umbrella stroller. If the stroller is mainly for airport use, the less weight you have to lug around the better. You can check your stroller in as you board the plane and pick it up on the way out. For parents who really like to be prepared, you can bring both. Many baby carriers are compact enough for easy stow away in your luggage. It's also a great option if you have more than one child and don't want to lug a double stroller.

3| Getting Through The Airport Faster With An Infant

Air travel isn't what it used to be. Thanks to the Federal Aviation Administration's ever-changing restrictions on what is allowed on an airplane, coupled with getting through security checkpoints; it's enough to fray the most seasoned traveler. By using these tried and true methods, you'll find getting through the airport and onto the plane might turn out to be a quick and painless process:

- Have your boarding passes ready and on hand before you get to the airport. You can print out your boarding passes 24 hours before your flight and go straight to the security clearance checkpoint.

- Always double check your flight's status before you leave the house and give yourself ample time to get to the airport.

- If you want to speed your way through the security checkpoint line, find out what the wait time is at each location by checking out the Transportation Security Administration's Website (www.tsa.dhs.gov).

- Even if the airline doesn't have a standard pre-boarding for parents with kids, it never hurts to ask. Most airport personnel will let you on the plane in the first tier of boarding passengers.

4| How To Save Money On A Flight

There's no doubt that travel can be pricey. When you're traveling as a family, you have to account for airfare and accommodations for everyone. The good news is that there are ways to make plane travel less expensive. Here are a few ways to help you save on travel:

- Be flexible. We realize this option isn't for everyone, but if you can move your departure date by a day or catch a later flight rather than an earlier one, you can find better deals. Use a travel search engine or a travel agent to help you find these deals.

- Book your flight mid-week. Specifically, flights tend to be less expensive on a Tuesday or Wednesday. The next least expensive flights tend to be on a Monday or Thursday. Invariably, weekend flights departing Friday through Sunday are usually the most expensive.

- If you can, book your flight during the off-season when less people will be traveling. For many locations, this may mean avoiding travel during the summer months (June, July, and August). A good way to double-check what time of the year is less expensive is by consulting a travel guide or travel agent for your destination.

· Sign up with an online travel newsletter. That way you'll know when good deals come around. Online travel newsletters like Travelzoo.com, and many of the travel sites like Expedia and Travelocity, will notify you of low airfares, last minute specials, package deals, accommodations and more. Family-Friendly Vacations (www.family-friendlyvacations.com) has a travel newsletter full of current deals geared just for family travel.

· Major search engines like Orbitz.com also give subscriber information on family travel specials.

Helpful Hint: There's an added bonus to booking your flight mid-week or off-season. If the flight is empty enough, you can have the whole plane row to yourself; more room for everyone, baby, and all your stuff!

5| Eight Ways to Make The Flight Go More Smoothly

We know flying on an airplane with infants in tow can be a daunting task. However, if you're prepared, you'll get through the whole process without a sweat. Let us give you the inside knowledge you need for a smooth flight:

1. Find out whether identification is needed to board the plane and whether they provide any disposable diapers or bibs. Check the airline's Website for more information or speak to an agent.

2. If you have the opportunity, choose your seats wisely when booking. The bulkhead seats are a popular choice with many parents. You get more legroom and airline bassinets can be hooked up to the bulkhead area of the plane. The drawback is that you won't have any under-seating storage in front of you. If you anticipate needing easy access to the plane's bathroom for diaper changes and clean-ups, or the need for some stretching and pacing, the rear of the plane is ideal for both.

3. Book your trip around baby's naptime. Consider whether the flight is a longer or shorter one, and whether your baby will do better napping on the plane or not; then plan accordingly.

4. Book a non-stop flight. It's a long enough journey between getting through security checkpoints, possible flight delays, and disembarking without worrying about layovers. Plus, if you miss a connecting flight due to a plane delay, you're in for a long, frustrating haul at the airport with your baby.

5. Bring along a toy or two for the trip. Something new and fascinating for baby as well as an old tried and true favorite will help alleviate at least some of the boredom your infant might experience.

6. Pack enough supplies for feeding, cleanup, and diaper changes. You don't want to be stuck on an 8-hour flight and have used up your last diaper 2 hours into the flight. Don't forget an extra change of clothes for baby and an extra shirt for you in case of baby spit-ups. Pack more if you're going on a long international flight.

7. When you book your child's ticket, reserve the kid's meal or infant food if the airline has it. If you have a toddler, you'll be glad to know the kid's meals get served in advance of regular meals. If you have an infant, certain major airline carriers do provide baby food, but you have to ask when you book.

8. For older infants, many parents swear by the DVD player. It's considered by some moms and dads to be a necessary evil, but if your child is toddler aged, DVD players with age appropriate movies and shows will keep them entertained for up to half an hour. We also like the laptop with DVD player idea. In addition to showing movies, you can play photo slideshows as well.

6| The Bare Essentials Plane Travel Pack List

Consider this familiar situation: you're hauling an oversized diaper bag on your shoulder that weighs more than your infant child. You've got a 30-pound stroller you're pushing and you're also carrying your baby over your shoulder. And you're doing all this just to go to the mall or the playground for an afternoon.

Parents have enough stuff to schlep around on a daily routine. Plane travel can compound the situation. The secret? Pack efficiently only using the bare minimum essentials. Here are some plane travel packing tips to help lighten your load:

- If you can manage it, don't check in your luggage. Just bring the requisite carry-ons to your flight. If it's a family trip, between you and your spouse, you should be able to survive a five-day trip with minimal luggage. Since you're usually limited to one carry-on and one personal item (check with your airline as rules are always changing), pack clothing and your personal essentials into your luggage.

- Your diaper bag, which should qualify as your personal item, should include feeding gear appropriate for your child's age:

  o Bottle or sippy cup

  o Formula or breast milk

  o Baby food or snacks

  o Utensils if you need them

  o Disposable bibs and pre-packed hand wipes

  o Diapers

  o Diaper wipes

  o Diaper cream

  o Large Zip-lock bags for soiled items

  o Medications

  o One change of clothes for baby

  o Requisite travel documents

  o Small toy or teething ring

Helpful Hint: Our rule of thumb: pack as much as you need to get to your destination and then add some extra. You want to walk the fine line between being prepared and packing the bare essentials. Remember, unless you're going to a remote location, you can always buy more of what you need at your destination.

7| Child Safety Seat Law

You know how important it is to have your infant in a car seat anytime your car is in motion. But beyond that, it's not only a safety issue …it's a legal issue. If you're traveling anywhere in the United States, you are required by law to have children up to three years of age ride in a child safety seat. Even more stringent are requirements in states like California and Oregon, which require children under six years in age or 60 pounds in weight to ride in appropriate child safety seats. Some states like New Jersey and North Carolina require car seats for a child who is under eight years old and under 80 pounds. Fines can vary state to state from $10 to $200. However, we think the repercussions of safety issues are much bigger than the fine you'll have to pay. If you're not sure what the requirements are for the state you live in or are traveling to, check with the Insurance Institute for Highway Safety (www.iihs.org) for comprehensive information.

8| Easy Transport For Your Baby Car Seat

If you've ever tried lugging your baby car seat from your living room out the door to your car, you're aware of just how bulky and cumbersome it is. Although it's an essential part of safety for travel on the road or plane, it's a heck of a pain to transport; unless you use one of these nifty ideas for convertible infant car seats.

- Turn your baby car seat into a stroller. It's possible with the use of an attachment such as the GoGo Kidz Travelmate. It's a lightweight, flat apparatus with a telescopic handle and razor wheels. You just screw the GoGo Kidz Travelmate to the back of your car seat, pull the handle, and go. It retails for about $90. Parents we know think the price is a bit steep, but well worth the ease of use and convenience.

- Use a car seat bag with wheels. We've heard good things about the Wheelie Car Seat Carrier by JL Childress. Put your car seat in, zip up the shaped bag, and attach it to your luggage or pull by the D-ring handle. Though your child can't sit in this one, it protects your car seat from dings when you're loading it in and out of the car, plane, or train.

9| The Car Seat and Taxi Dilemma

Does this scenario sound familiar? You have to get to and from the airport in a taxi, but you don't want to tote 20 pounds of car seat with you. According to the American Automobile Club of California, transportation vehicles like taxi cabs and shuttles don't have the same requirements that passenger vehicles have for child safety seats. State laws regarding putting a car seat in a taxi do vary. For instance, in Massachusetts, it's the parent's responsibility to provide a car seat, although drivers can be fined. However, requirements are one thing and safety is another. You do have some alternatives.

- Use a limousine service and hire out a town car or stretch limo. Some places do have car seats, so you'll have to check around.

- Call various taxi cab companies. Many do not carry car seats, but there are a few out there that do. If you find one, use them.

- Call in a favor from a trusted friend or relative and have them drop you off and pick you up from the airport.

- For toddlers, there is a product available called the Tote N Go Portable car seat. If you have an older infant or toddler who is at least 25 pounds, it's an affordable purchase that meets federal car seat standards.

10| Have Baby Car Seat, Will Travel

Baby car seats are an important safety item for trips in the car as well as on the plane. We're assuming most of you already have an infant car seat or convertible car seat for your baby, but in case you're prepping for travel and wondering what's appropriate for your child, read on.

- Kids' car seats come in three versions: infant car seats, convertible car seats, and booster seats. Knowing the differences in each will help you decide what to buy. Convertible car seats might have longer-term use from the get-go, but consider starting with a rear-facing infant car seats which detaches from its base and come with a handle. They're better designed to accommodate a young infant or newborn's frame. And you'll be able to detach it from its base so when you have a sleeping infant, you won't have to take your baby out of the seat; a process that could very well wake her up. Many infant car seats accommodate up to 22 pounds in weight and 26 inches in height.

- Convertible infant car seats work best for older infants and toddlers. As a rule of thumb, keep him rear-facing until your infant is at least 20 pounds and over one year old.

- Don't assume that the more expensive car seats are necessarily better. What you tend to get with higher priced infant car seats are shock absorbent foam, upgraded fabrics, and user-friendlier seat adjustability. However, all car seats must meet minimum safety standards as mandated by the federal government. If you're concerned about safety, EPS foam, no-twist straps, a five-point harness, and the use of a tether in a car seat does make riding in the car safer for your infant.

- Check the safety crash test ratings of an infant car seat. One place to check is the Consumer Reports Web site.

- Check the weight and height requirements of the seat. Some have weight limits right at 22 pounds while others max out at 20 pounds. Many infant car seats accommodate babies up to 26", but some accommodate babies up to 30" in height.

- Find out what the weight of the actual seat is. When you're carrying around an infant car seat that weighs over ten pounds with a ten-pound baby in it, you might just wish you picked a lighter car seat.

11| Toddlers And Car Seats

Riding unrestrained in a car is the biggest cause of death and injury among children. Want to hear a sobering statistic? In 2004, 50 percent of the deaths in kids younger than 14 were caused by accidents where kids were not using safety restraints while in their vehicles. Follow these tips on toddler car seats to protect your child from harm in an automobile.

- If you have a toddler, she most likely should be in a convertible car seat. The best time to turn toddler car seats forward is when your little one is at least a year old and more than 20 pounds.

- Use the LATCH system or the seat belt to restrain car seats in your vehicle. A car seat should move no more than an inch in either direction.

- If your car seat has a tether and your car can accommodate it, it's a good idea to use it. A tether will limit the forward motion of a car seat in the event of a crash.

- When your toddler's shoulders are above the top slots of the car seat, she's outgrown it. Most children outgrow their car seats around four or five years of age.

12| Everything You Want To Know About Car Seats

If you want to get the low-down on which car seats are better to install or how to make travel with car seats safer for your baby, try one of these Websites.

National Highway Traffic Safety Administration (www.nhtsa.dot.gov) - Go here to find the latest guidelines and news about car seat safety. Concerned about product recalls? You can find that info here, too.

Safe Kids Worldwide (www.safekids.org) - Their site contains some great safety information on the basic requirements for infant car seats. If you need some statistics to help you appreciate the value of a good car seat, you can find it on their site as well.

American Academy of Pediatrics (www.aap.org) - They are an excellent resource for what's safe and what's not for infants, toddlers, and children in child safety restraint systems. Their comprehensive car seat guides should tell you just about everything you want to know about keeping your child safe in a motor vehicle. You can also find a guide to many of the products available on the market.

CarSeatData.org (www.carseatdata.org) - If you want to find a car seat safety technician near you or just want to know if a car seat is compatible with your car, they have a large database from which you can do your research.

13| Your Infant Car Seat And The Rental Car

There are some instances when lugging around your infant car seat is just not convenient or practical. However, you can get around without taking your own car seat with you everywhere. When you rent a car, you can also rent a car seat for your infant or toddler. Rates vary, but they usually range from five to 10 dollars per day on top of your normal car rental fee. Be prepared to tell them the age and weight of your infant so they can select the appropriate model. Since you won't have your usual infant car seat, there are a few things you can do to check on the safety of the car seats.

- Inquire which models of car seats the rental company uses.
- Find out the model year.
- Ask how often they replace the car seats.
- Find out what criteria, if any, they have for replacing them.

If you're concerned about the safety ratings, check the Consumer Reports Website (www.consumerreports.org) for their latest crash test ratings.

Helpful Hint: You have another option besides renting car seats from rental car agencies if you're not satisfied with what they have to offer. A number of companies offer car seat rentals, among other baby items. Baby's Away is one major rental equipment service provider with locations throughout the United States that rents car seats and other baby items.

14| Baby Carriers For Carrying Young Ones and Newborns

Baby carriers are a wonderful way to tote younger babies and newborns around. Parents get to have their hands free and babies get to be close to Mom or Dad. With younger infants, you should keep in mind the necessity for neck support when choosing a carrier.

For easy on, easy off carriers for younger babies and newborns, try a pouch. They're relatively simple to wear and place baby in. Just put a sling over one shoulder, tuck your infant in safely, and you're ready to go. Babies can be worn in front or back. Get one in the right fabric and color, and dads likely won't mind wearing this one to carry baby around in.

Slings are also good for younger babes, too. However, they require a bit more work in the beginning because having greater flexibility to carry your child in different positions also means figuring out what works best. Until your infant is at least a year old, wear baby in front with a sling. Soft front carriers are another great option for the youngest of infants.

The appearance of most soft-front carriers appeal to both Mom and Dad. *Baby Bjorn* makes one which works nicely for infants starting at eight pounds and 21 inches. For travel and carrying your little one for extensive periods, we recommend getting the *Baby Bjorn Active Carrier* version. The added lumbar support will remove a lot of weight off your shoulders.

15| A Baby Carrier That Does Double Duty

Just when we thought we'd seen just about every type of baby carrier out there, we found one that doubles as a baby carrier and backpack. You can carry younger infants on your front and tote around essentials on your back. These baby carriers are made by Sherpani. You can choose from two models: The Sherpani Emi ($65) and the Sherpani Emi V2 ($95).

The main difference is that the V2 model comes with a removable daypack, so you can choose to just carry baby and use the pack as a sling instead. Both versions come with a cozy fleece lined material to keep babies comfy and a tube sleeve for moms who want to hydrate on the go. The packs look sporty enough that we think dads would be as happy wearing them as moms.

16| Best Baby Carriers For Nursing On The Go

If you're nursing and traveling, one way to keep baby close to you and facilitate easy nursing is by the use of a suitable baby carrier. Which baby carriers are best for nursing, you ask? While we don't think there is any one best bet, many baby-wearing aficionados do feel the slings and pouches make nursing easier. The sling is a loop of fabric with the ability to adjust the size and fit at the shoulder for a custom fit. Smaller infants stay cradled in the sling and you can carry her on the front, back, or hip. Slings come padded for extra comfort or without for maximum portability. There are a lot of great ones, but we like:

Ella Roo Baby Slings ($50 and up) great fabrics, just a bit of padding, and not too much bulky fabric. The pouch is another favorite among baby wearers. These baby carriers are just like the slings without the adjustability. The upside is you have a carrier you can easily pack away into your diaper bag or luggage. Hotslings ($45-$80) for their fashion forward fabrics. Plus they come with just a wee bit of give for added comfort.

Helpful Hint: To make your sling or pouch more comfortable, sizing is key. The bottom of your infant should end up between your hip and your belly-button.

17| Structured Backpack Carriers For Hiking

If you're heading to the great outdoors with baby in tow, consider a structured backpack tailor-made for long hikes and sheltering your child from the harsh sun or inclement weather. Before you imagine you're going to be lugging around a hefty outdoor carrier plus a small child, listen to this: you can get a relatively lightweight structured backpack carrier. There are a number of models on the market with lightweight aluminum frames. Take a look at the Kelty backpacks - designed for taking your infant on some outdoor excursions.

The Kelty Pathfinder ($190) is a mid-line model that's popular with fans of the Kelty brand. It weighs just over seven pounds, making it easier to take your child on an outdoor hike. Contoured shoulder straps and a molded padded belt help ensure your comfort, while a sun and rain hood helps keep your little one protected from the elements.

Sherpani also has two structured backpack carriers that parents are pleased with. The Sherpani brand is geared for women, but the structured carriers are designed for both men and women in mind. The Sherpani Rumba Superlight baby carrier is a great buy for $150 and weighs just over four pounds without accessories, while the $205 Rumba Unisex baby carrier is for those who want a bigger storage capacity.

18| Top Picks For Toddler Carriers

Toddlers are the perfect candidates for a backpack carrier. They can get a nice view of the surroundings while enjoying a lift from a parent. And neck muscle control isn't a concern; a requirement for a youngster riding backpack-style in a soft carrier.

To get the most mileage out of a toddler carrier, get one you can wear in multiple ways. When traveling, if you anticipate navigating a lot of stairs and crowded areas or simply prefer the use of a baby carrier, try some of these favorites.

For soft carriers, try the *Ergo Baby Carrier* ($90-$100). Some carriers will give you strain after half an hour of use. This one should keep you and your little one comfortable for quite a while. This cotton canvas carrier comes full of features like a zippered pocket, padded shoulder straps, and a hood for your little one. You can carry younger infants in front and older tots in the back. It's rugged enough for a hike outdoors and works equally well if you're zipping through the airport.

Another favorite is the *Beco Baby Carrier*, created by an active, outdoorsy mother who was determined to create a comfortable carrier for taking her son out and about with her. Fabric choices like crane patterns over a swath of blossoms or a funky dot print make these carriers much more chic. They're great for back carries, but you can use them for front carries and hip carries as well.

19| Your Guide To Baby Carriers

If you're getting ready to travel with an infant, baby carriers are an indispensable tool. Even if you're not traveling and just trying to accomplish a few things around the house, baby carriers make parents' lives easier. If you're planning on getting one for your trip, take heed of these baby carrier tips.

Baby carriers come in all sorts of shapes, sizes, and fabrics. Here's the lowdown on some of the more common as well as lesser-known styles.

Backpack carriers: Great for toting around older infants and toddlers, you essentially wear baby on your back. Typically, babies face you. They should be able to sit unsupported on their own and have solid neck control.

Hip Carrier: The weight rests on one shoulder and on your hip. You'll likely use these with older babies and toddlers.

Pouches: They come in all kinds of fabrics; some with give in them and some without. They're a one-piece loop of fabric which opens up to create a pouch for baby. You can use pouches for newborns up to toddlers, but most folks use them for younger babes.

Soft Front Carriers: Wear your baby in the front, either facing you or facing out. These carriers tend to work well for younger babies and children under one.

Slings: It's just like the pouch, but with the flexibility of an adjustable ring or device at the shoulder to create a proper fit.

Traditional Baby Carriers: They're modeled after the traditional Asian baby carriers. *The Mei Tai* and *Podegi* are two examples of traditional Asian baby carriers. They come in great fabrics and are very versatile. There is a learning curve to use these, though, so beginners take note.

Wraparound baby carriers: Characterized by lots of fabric, wraparound baby carriers allow the wearer to literally wrap several yards of fabric into a comfy nesting spot for baby.

20| Six Beach Activities To Keep Little Ones Entertained

Besides the calming sounds of lapping waves hitting the shore and enjoying the warmth of a sun-kissed day, there are a few other reasons we enjoy beach vacations with infants. Beaches come built-in as outdoor entertainment centers for little ones. Besides you, and a good dose of sun block, there's not much else a young child needs to keep her occupied at the beach. Still, we've put together a few ways you can enjoy your time at the beach with baby.

1. Create your own mini moat by digging a trench in the sand and adding water. Make sure you keep baby supervised at all times.

2. Build your own sandcastle tower and let your tot be the bulldozer.

3. Camp out on a beach towel under an umbrella and bring along a few baby toys for play. The view of the ocean and folks passing by will be enough to keep older infants and toddlers entertained.

4. Pull out the jogging stroller and take your little one for a run along the strand. It's one ride that just might lull her to sleep.

5. Take out the baby carrier and go for a stroll along the sand. You can enjoy the cool breeze and baby gets to enjoy the ride.

6. For toddlers and older babies, toss a beach ball along the edge of the water. We bet just watching the waves come in will be entertainment enough.

21| Traveling Solo With Baby

If you're a single parent or just heading out on a trip with baby on your own, rest assured that getting to your destination is not only doable, it can be a great, liberating experience. In case you're planning out your journey with some trepidation, we've put together some helpful hints to ease your worries.

- Pack the bare minimum. Especially if you're going by plane, you only want to pack the essentials you'll need to get you through the trip. Think long and hard before you decide to lug that portable crib with you. Maybe you borrow one at your destination or can you rent one for use when you arrive. It helps to be prepared, but when you're transporting an infant and 35 pounds of gear, you might think some things were best left at home.

- Plan your route. If you're going by plane, identify your gate terminal, connecting flights, and destination as much as possible beforehand, rather than scrambling around to find out where you're going as you're trying to soothe your cranky infant. If you're driving, figure out where your rest stops will be ahead of time, so you don't end up stopping in the middle of nowhere to tend to baby.

- Bring hands-free gear. Whatever you can do to keep your hands as free as possible, do so. Use a baby carrier so you can have hands free for your luggage or carry your luggage in a backpack if you're going to use a stroller.

- Put it all on wheels. Don't lug around that fancy leather overnight bag when you can pull luggage much more easily on wheels. The less weight you'll have to bear, the better. This includes items like the car seat as well; put it in a bag, get a wheeled attachment, or get a convertible car seat stroller.

- Elicit the help of others. Traveling on your own is no time to be shy. If you need someone to help you put your luggage in the overhead compartment so baby doesn't fall out of her still unstrapped infant seat, do so.

- Keep documents in one place. Passports, boarding passes, identification, and other papers should all be in one easy-to-reach place so you're not fishing for them while trying to keep one arm around your sleeping child.

- Keep in touch. Let friends and family members know your itinerary and where and when they should expect you to be.

- Keep an open mind. Traveling with young children can be challenging; more so if you're doing it on your own. But expect the best and be prepared for the worst and you'll do just fine.

22| Go Disney: On A Cruise

Many parents can't wait to take their baby or toddler on a trip to an amusement park. We think theme parks are great ideas for family vacations. But until babies are older, they're really for parents' enjoyment. One alternative to visiting Mickey at the theme park is to go on a Disney Cruise. Granted, you could be paying a grand more than you would on other ships for a week-long cruise, but the level of service and amenities on Disney Cruise ships keep it booked solid, according to an article in a recent *Frommer's* newsletter.

Disney cruises have virtually something for every parent, from a three-night Bahamas cruise to 14-night Transatlantic journey that'll take you to Spain. These are just a few of the features you can expect to get when you sail with Mickey:

- Art Deco Style cabins that give you some of the largest square footage around. Their outside cabins boast 214 square feet of space, while you'd be lucky to get 200 square feet of space on another cruise line's comparable cabin.

- Toddlers under three years old can go with a parent to play on a jumbo-sized pirate ship.

- Ships have a shallow pool area for toddlers and babies in swim diapers, while other cruise lines do not.

- Everyone gets to experience life-sized Disney characters on board like Mickey, Minnie, and Goofy.

- Themed family-friendly restaurants, including one modeled after a parrot jungle.
- Separate entertainment just for grown-ups such as a comedy club and piano bar.
- Disney character musical productions the whole family can enjoy.
- Shorefront drop-off to a private island for Disney cruise ship patrons.

23| Theme Parks With Baby

Some parents simply cannot wait to take their children to a theme park. If your child is still uttering words sounding like "Gah" or "Coo", we suspect the theme park experience is more for you than for baby. Though your visit won't be quite the way it was before baby arrived, here are a few suggestions on taking your little one to a theme park.

- Don't plan too much in a day. If you've booked a nearby hotel, you can take a few days to explore the major theme parks.

- Bring a stroller or rent one. For smaller babies, consider a baby carrier. If your infant will sleep in the stroller or carrier, you can take some time out to relax. Take a stroll through the shops or find a more scenic area of the park to enjoy.

- A number of theme parks have baby care centers. Baby care centers are cozy places where you can change diapers, breastfeed your baby, or kick up your heels with baby in a rocker.

- Theme parks also come with long lines. A number of theme parks offer a fast pass service. This pass allows you to go explore other areas of the park until your designated time. You then get to speed through the line to get on a ride.

Helpful Hint: If you have a toddler-aged child, consider Legoland in Carlsbad, California, which has toddler-appropriate rides and attractions. Sesame Place, which is in Longhorn, Pennsylvania, is a theme park with water attractions that tots will enjoy as well.

24| All-Inclusive Vacations With Baby

Have you been dreaming of relaxing on the sandy shores of Ixtapa, Mexico? Or perhaps exploring the terrain around Saint Ambroggio in France is more your style. Sound impossible with an infant? Not quite. With an all-inclusive vacation, you can visit exotic locales, take baby with you, and be able to enjoy some much needed couple time. All-inclusive vacations are self-contained resort areas. The complete package generally includes accommodations, food, beverages, and activities. In the case of family-friendly all inclusive vacations, you get the added bonus of available childcare and programs for babies, children and teens.

According to Staci Blunt, owner of Family Friendly Vacations, the best all inclusive vacation resorts are those run by *Beaches* and *Club Med,* simply because they do have programs that cater to families. In fact, Club Med provides pre-screened childcare for infants as young as 4 months old. *Beaches* has certified nannies for babies of all ages; even newborns. On that note, we'd be pretty surprised to find a mother ready to vacation with her newborn.

25| So Many Resorts, So Little Time

There are a number of different all inclusive resort locations you can try. But keep in mind not all of them have childcare and programs for children and infants. If you have your sights set on a tropical vacation, there are a number of locations throughout North and South America as well as Europe to choose from.

Club Med (www.clubmed.com) has several resorts especially geared towards families. These Club Med vacations have Baby Club Med programs for infants from 4 to 23 months. For an extra daily fee of $40 per day, you can place your infant in childcare programs with CPR trained nannies. Parents have given us rave reviews on Club Meds in Ixtapa, Mexico, Cancun, Mexico, and Punta Cana, Dominican Republic. The Club Med Cancun has had a recent remodel and word is that it's quite nice!

Beaches (www.beaches.com) resorts are all geared towards families. They also provide nannies who are certified child development specialists through accredited U.S. university programs. Their youngest program caters to newborns through toddlers up to 23 months old. *Beaches* has some well regarded locations in the Caribbean, including Jamaica, Negril, and Turks and Caicos. If you're looking for a more upscale setting, some folks find the Beaches resorts to be a bit more luxurious in general.

26| Family Camps for the Whole Gang

It's possible to have pre-planned activities, meals, lodging, childcare, and a family atmosphere in an outdoor setting. Consider family camps. Family camps are like summer camp for the whole family. If you're looking for a vacation where you can enjoy the outdoors and have a program in place for all your children, family camps might be one vacation you should start planning.

Shady Creek Family Camp & Conference Center – It's in the foothills of the Sierra Mountains in California near the Yuba River. You'll find access to a host of outdoor activities like archery, boating, and hiking. If you're really daring, try the "Leap of Faith" rope course; you'll climb over 55 feet high in the trees, walk onto a plank, and take a 10-foot leap to catch a trapeze bar. Accommodations aren't too shabby, either. Take your pick from mountain cabins with a view, unique dome-shaped cabins modeled after Native American dwellings, or stay at their Crescent Lodge. And yes, there are programs for infants and individual babysitting, as well.

Santa Barbara Family Vacation Center – Located on the University of Santa Barbara (UCSB) campus, this family camp is great for the sports-minded family. Choose from activities like biking, surfing, golfing, and kayaking. In the evening, enjoy on-site activities or go for a night out on the town in Santa Barbara. At night, retire to one of UCSB's campus accommodations which boast two to four-bedroom suites. Infants as young as a month old have childcare and can stay in their own room during naptime. For more locations throughout the country, check out some of the YMCA family camps.

27| The City Trip

The city trip is a good bet because you'll have access to everything you need at your destination. You can be the tourist and go sightseeing, or live like one of the locals and immerse yourself in a neighborhood for a week. So where does one go for a city trip? Here are some suggestions for our two favorite baby city spots: New York and San Francisco.

New York – New York is jam-packed with restaurants and shops on nearly every corner and block – all within walking distance of your stay. Take your stroller with you and explore with your infant. Stay at the Doubletree Guest Suites, which has two-room suites that are perfect for families. Besides the fact that cribs, strollers, and childproofing is offered, you can just walk out and stroll by landmarks like Radio City Music Hall and Rockefeller Center.

San Francisco – Older children and toddlers will enjoy visits to Golden Gate Park where they can enjoy the gardens, ponds, and ducks. A stay at The W San Francisco is worth your while if you're traveling here. You don't have to sacrifice style at this swanky hotel that just happens to be part of a family-friendly group of W Hotels. Cribs and references for babysitting services are available upon request.

Helpful Hint: To find everything and anything there is to do in a city with kids, visit www.gocitykids.com and go to the city you'll be visiting. They've got indoor activities, outdoor activities, classes, museums, and seasonal events listed by an age appropriate category. It's a great way to plan your trip or find something spontaneous to do.

28| Tyler Place Family Resort

How does a trip out to an all-inclusive resort where you can bike, canoe, or windsurf while trained childcare staff tends to baby sound? Such a place does exist in the U.S. at the Tyler Place Family Resort. Set amidst 165 acres of land in Highgate Springs, Vermont, the Tyler Place Family Resort is a family-owned facility that has been around since 1933. In addition to the numerous sports offerings like volleyball, soccer, basketball, yoga, and racquetball, parents have the option for evenings out with live music, bonfires, and organized social events. For those who enjoy water activities, take the whole gang out on a leisurely paddleboat ride or take a sailing lesson. There's something for kids and the littlest of babies, as well. They have programs for newborns through teens.

Programs for babies up to 18 months of age include the availability of a parent's helper, age-appropriate play activities, and developmental toys. You can leave the portable crib and high chairs at home as well because they have just about every item and piece of equipment you could need at your stay. Families are so enamored with the Tyler Place Family Resort, they tend to come back year after year, so if you want to go, you'll have to book far in advance. For more information on rates and when you can stay, check out their Website at www.tylerplace.com.

29| Family-Friendly Accommodations For Baby

When you're traveling with an infant, you want to stay at accommodations that are family-friendly. Read on to find out just what to look for and where you can find some great places to stay for your next family vacation.

Family-friendly accommodations include hotels which have some or all of offer the following:

- Free hotel stays for kids under 18
- Rooms with suites and kitchens to accommodate families
- Complimentary cribs, strollers, baby shampoo, and bottle warmers
- Childproofing upon request
- In-room baby-sitting

If you're wondering where to look for accommodations that will make you and baby feel right at home, it's usually a safe bet to check with hotels around family resort areas like Orlando, Florida and Anaheim, California. You'll find an abundance of places to stay which cater specifically to families. Some hotel chains are composed almost entirely of suites. Typically, you'll find family-friendly accommodations among the following hotel chains:

- Holiday Inn
- Residence Inn by Marriott
- Embassy Suites
- Loews Hotels
- Hyatt Resorts

Helpful Hint: Besides the bigger hotels, try condo rentals, vacation home rentals, cabins, and bed and breakfasts for accommodations that can be family-friendly.

LifeTips.com > > Baby Friendly Vacations

30| Family Travel Heats Up

If you're considering family travel, you're in good company. According to a nationwide poll across the U.S., nearly 80% of travel agents cited family travel as the fastest climbing travel trend. Though we know those of you who are interested in taking baby with you on a trip probably aren't thinking about exposing your child to different cultures and customs – other parents are. Travel agents cited that travel was on the rise because parents wanted to teach their kids about the lifestyles in other countries. Of course, the bonding experience that comes along with travel is a strong point for going on a trip as well.

So what does that mean for you, as the parent of an infant? It means that for 2007 and beyond, if you're thinking about booking at popular locations or during the summer months, book early! Staci Blunt of Family Friendly Travel recommends you plan six months in advance whenever possible. For the holidays, you might want to consider planning even farther ahead if you can. If you're traveling in the off-season, that's when you don't have to plan as far ahead. In that case, Ms. Blunt feels planning three months ahead of time is a safe bet.

31| Going On The Babymoon

Everyone knows what a honeymoon is, but now there's the "babymoon." The "babymoon" was coined due to the increasing number of couples who decide to take a vacation right before baby arrives …as sort of a last "hurrah" before parenthood. Babymoons typically refer to trips taken in the second and third trimester of a couple's pregnancy. And it's not necessarily a marketing gimmick from the travel industry.

According to a research study done by Liberty Travel, nearly 60% of expectant couples surveyed took a planned trip before baby's arrival. So if you're thinking about planning that last getaway before baby's arrival, you're in good company.

32| Some Inspiration For Your Babymoon Getaway

The travel industry says more couples are packing their bags and going on a trip before baby arrives. This may be as simple as an overnight getaway or a week-long resort stay. We think it's a good idea, too. Couples can spend some quality time together, getting away from it all before the arrival of baby. We've got a few sample ideas for those of you contemplating one last getaway.

Some hotels have offered packages specifically geared toward the babymooning couple. For instance, the *St. Regis Hotel* has offered a "Last Hurrah" package complete with themed DVDs, his and hers massages, and a "cravings menu" for those late night snacks. To locate such a package near you, contact your travel agent.

Another route to take is to create your own sample package. Book your own romantic getaway to a place like *Carmel By The Sea*. Stay at the historic *Cypress Inn*, book reservations at the charming *Casanova Restaurant*, and spend your days visiting the shops and relaxing on the beach. Go tropical to a Caribbean vacation. *The Peter Island Resort* in the Caribbean can offer both parents-to-be spa treatments, a beachfront suite, and miles of sand. Enjoy a picnic outside and enjoy the relaxing tranquility of turquoise waters, shady palm trees, and white beaches.

33| Great Picks For Family-Friendly Stays

Some places claim to be family-friendly. But there's more to offering accommodations that are receptive to folks with babies and kids than merely allowing them to stay. We've found a few places you'll have a hard time leaving because the establishment really goes out of its way to make the kids happy. Here they are:

The Bed and Breakfast: Not every bed and breakfast is family-friendly, but for those who like the intimate service and character, it's a perfect choice if the owners welcome children with open arms. Try the Holly Tree Inn, located in Point Reyes, California. Book one of their child-friendly cottages and then switch off childcare with your spouse for an appointment with the masseuse.

The Upscale Hotel: Going to an upscale hotel immediately conjures images of upturned noses at children running afoot and babies having a meltdown. But there are some high-end hotels which do embrace children. The Four Seasons Hotel New York has great perks like free stays for kids under 18, childproofing upon request, and the use of free cribs, strollers, and bottle warmers.

The Resort: Having a baby doesn't mean staying at a resort is out of the question, especially when it's a resort catering to families. Woodloch Pine Resort in Hawley, Pennsylvania, offers just about something for everyone in the family. Think of it as a resort with the activities that a full-scale outdoor camp would offer. Choose your stay at a standard room or splurge with guest home accommodations. Kids under 3 stay free as long as they're rooming with two adults.

34| Four Not-So-Family-Friendly Vacations

Though we trust you all have a keen sense of judgment when it comes to deciding what trip would and wouldn't be appropriate for your infant, we thought we'd throw in our list of four otherwise great vacations that aren't family-friendly.

Maybe you've always been the adventurous type and you just loathe to give up the high adrenaline lifestyle. More power to you! However, if your vacation involves scaling sheer cliffs, trekking sub freezing temperatures, and approaching arctic wildlife, it's not a family-friendly vacation.

We think beach vacations and the bustle of travelers coming together to celebrate a new season is a terrific ritual. Cancun is a resort town with stunning beaches and an active nightlife. However, travel during spring break with an infant in tow when the area is teeming with partygoers; not a good family vacation.

A trip out to China to see 11 cities in 14 days complete with 10 planned daytrips sounds like a culture enriching once in a lifetime experience. However, it's hard enough for grown-ups to make it through such a whirlwind adventure, let alone an infant who has round the clock feeding and sleeping needs.

A road trip from coast to coast through deserts, mountains, small towns, farm lands, and urban cities in a week can be a blast, if you don't have to worry about stopping for feedings, changing diapers, and setting aside naptimes.

35| Say Aloha, Baby!

Warm waters. Tropical breezes. And all the modern conveniences to make your trip comfortable. If it sounds as good to you as it does to us, plan a trip with your baby to Hawaii. But don't just pick any island or location. There are a few that are perfect for bringing little ones in tow.

Ka'anapali Beach – Located on the western part of Maui, it's a great place for families with a baby. You can have access to white, sandy beaches, and gentle waves – perfect for taking little ones. Not only that, you'll be visiting a resort area with renowned snorkeling opportunities. Ka'anapali Beach topped the list during 2003 as America's Best Beach, according to Dr. Stephen P. Leatherman. Stay at one of the luxury hotels or make your home away from home at family-friendly condo rental.

Baby Beach – This area is another great find on the western shores of the island of Maui. The calm waters on Baby Beach make it a popular area for families with little ones. A protected area keeps waves from crashing in and the flat stretch of sandy area makes it ideal for tots. Parents can choose vacation home rentals or resort hotel accommodations and everything in between.

36| The Snow Trip

Just because you have an infant doesn't mean you have to kiss your snow trips goodbye. In fact, if you go to a family-friendly resort with childcare in place, both Mom and Dad will be able to hit the slopes. Not sure where to go?

Try **Whistler Blackcomb** in British Columbia, Canada. Besides the opportunity to ski or snowboard on over 8,000 acres of snow on a renowned ski resort, you also have access to a vast array of restaurants from pizzerias to French cuisine. Families can choose from just about every type of accommodation available – large hotels, bed and breakfasts, condos, and vacation homes are abundant in the area. Many of them are within walking distance to shops, places to eat, and skiing gondolas.

The best part? CPR certified early childhood educators will watch your kids who are anywhere from three months to four years old. Because of the popularity of the childcare program, parents do have to reserve a spot early, so it's best to plan your trip as far in advance as possible.

37| The Zoo Alternative

The zoo can be a wonderful educational experience for young children and adults alike. But there is an alternative to taking your little ones to the zoo.

For young toddlers and infants, a trip out to a butterfly habitat is an even better idea. You'll enter a world surrounded by vibrant colors and lots of motion – two things babies and toddlers love. Don't know where to go? Here are a few ideas for a stopover on your next trip.

Butterfly Pavilion (www.butterflies.org)– Located in Westminster, Colorado, the Butterfly Pavilion is actually an insect zoo. Not only do they have 1,200 butterflies from around the globe, the 30,000 square foot facility houses tarantulas and scorpions as well as sea urchins, turtles, and fish.

Mackinac Island Butterfly House (www.originalbutterflyhouse.com)– This Mackinac Island, Michigan butterfly facility has 1,800 square feet of space to house 40 species of butterflies amid a tropical garden. In addition, there is an exotic insect display featuring larger-than-life insects like the Rhino Beetle and 14" Walking Stick.

Butterfly Conservatory (www.niagaraparks.com)- Located a few minutes from the famous Niagara Falls, there are over 2,000 butterflies in a rainforest setting. Visitors walk along a 600-foot pathway to view over 50 species of butterflies in a warm, climate-controlled environment.

38| Three Not-So-Obvious Baby Spots

If you're in the city and trying to come up with some ideas for where to take your infant for a few hours, there are an abundance of places that are tailor made just for you and baby. Going out to the park or out for a stroll are just a few ideas, but these places do welcome babies, too:

The Library - Many parents might imagine hushed silences and stern librarians when they think of libraries. However, many libraries do, in fact, welcome babies and even have children's sections stocked with plush animals for younger tots and babies as well. The best time to go is during a storytelling session geared just for babies and toddlers. Check with the local library in the area to find out just when they occur.

The Movie Theater – It's true. Movie theaters are baby-appropriate zones, at least during designated days and times during the week. Theaters like Loews and Mann in some cities have opened up their facilities to accommodate parents with infants who want to watch a current film on the big screen. Though you'll have to contend with the sound of crying babies, no one will care if your own baby makes any noise.

The Yoga Studio- It's not quite the same as having a meditative moment on your own, but it can be a fun and relaxing way to bond with your child. A number of yoga studios have programs incorporating classes for moms and babies. For the Pilate's fan, try a class created for you and baby.

39| Friendly Activities By Stroller

If you're trying to decide where to take your toddler out around town, there's no better way to go than a stroller if you pick the right venues. Whether you're visiting a new locale for a few days or looking for someplace to spend the afternoon, here are some ideas for parents looking for some stroller-friendly places to go.

1. Go on a walking tour. With a young child in tow, you don't necessarily want to join the crowd. Map out your own route or try one by cell phone. Talking Street is one company that offers cell phone tours in several cities throughout the U.S.

2. Join a fitness group. You can sign up for just the day to get a workout with child in tow. Stroller Strides (www.strollerstrides.com) and StrollerFit (www.strollerfit.com) have numerous locations to choose from.

3. Go on a hike. You'll need a stroller that can handle the terrain and not every hiking trail can accommodate a stroller, but there are some that do. Check with the local Parks and Recreation Department to find out which ones do. It's a great way to enjoy the fresh air and scenic view.

4. Explore the local neighborhood. It's easy to miss all the nuances of a community when you're going by car. Whether you're in your hometown or vacationing in a resort town, it's a refreshing experience to take a walk on foot.

5. Go to a botanical garden. Tots and parents alike will enjoy the landscaped environments, colorful flowers, and serene environment that a lush botanical garden has to offer.

40| How To Pick A Stroller For Travel

Keeping in mind that there is no one dream stroller out there that is best for every type of situation, we think you can still use some reasonable judgment and a set of good criteria to get the best stroller for your travel needs.

Whether you've got one trip in mind or you're planning for outings throughout the year, we think asking yourself this set of questions will help you figure out what's best for you.

1. What kind of trip are you planning? Are you going by car or traveling by plane? *Hint:* This will tell you what kind of restrictions you need on your stroller selection, such as size and weight.

2. What will you be using your stroller for? Are you just getting from one place to another or will you be jogging? *Hint:* You can hone in on different types of strollers, like lightweight strollers, all-terrain strollers, or jogging strollers.

3. What type of ground will you encounter? Will there be paved streets or will there be rough roads? *Hint:* This will tell you whether you need to look for a solid stroller with suspension or whether you can get away with an umbrella stroller for travel.

4. What will the weather be like? Will it be warm and humid or cold and rainy? *Hint:* You can figure out whether you need a canopy and other protective covering for your infant.

5. What's the age and weight of your infant? *Hint*: Certain strollers aren't appropriate for younger infants. For instance, joggers are more appropriate for older infants with good neck muscle control. Check the weight restrictions of a particular model of stroller.

6. How much are you willing to spend? *Hint*: Your budget will be the ultimate determinant of what you can and can't buy. Remember not to get carried away with the lure of features you don't need. But it's important not to make a decision solely on cost savings.

Something to think about: A $700 pram stroller with an aluminum chassis, luxury foot muff, mosquito net, and diaper bag with changing pad might not be what you need for a trek through the airport. On the flip side, a $50 umbrella stroller doesn't have the durability of one that costs $300. If you expect to use an inexpensive stroller on a week-long jaunt through bumpy sidewalks on an urban road, re-think the inexpensive stroller purchase.

41| The Beach Stroller

Headed out for the beach this summer and planning on bringing a stroller? If you are, it's important to remember that most strollers aren't made to withstand getting inundated with sand and salt water. If your wheels are made of steel, they'll rust due to salt water. Even if they're aluminum, the sand will tend to jam the wheels. If you're going to take your stroller out to the beach, the best thing to do is stay on a clean pathway. However, if you must go out to sandy terrain, there is one jogging stroller that will navigate the ground with ease. The Kool Stride Senior has sealed bearings to keep the sand out. Get the alloy version and you'll find the 20" rear wheels and 16" front wheel will cover sandy ground without damage to the stroller. If you're taking this one for travel, pop off the wheels and fold up the canvas frame for maximum portability.

42| One Size Doesn't Fit All Travel Strollers

Contrary to the notion that you should pack light, Strollerqueen Janet McLaughlin, who runs a service recommending the best stroller for parents of babies and toddlers, recommends you throw out that idea and look at what you'll be doing on the trip instead. According to Strollerqueen, it's not always a good idea to pack light when you're picking out the best stroller for travel. For instance, if you're taking a road trip to San Francisco, you want a stroller that can handle walks up and down the hills and streets of the city. On the flip side, if you're taking a stroller to a foreign city, where the streets are unpaved or made of cobblestone, petite wheels and an umbrella stroller will not survive your trip.

A stroll on the beach requires a stroller that can handle the gritty beach and not all strollers can do that. In a nutshell, there really is no one-size-fits-all stroller for travel. A little research goes a long way. If you're in the market for a new stroller for your travels, you can do some investigation to find out which one would hold up best under rugged terrain or work fine for city streets.

Baby Bargains by Denise & Alan Fields has a fairly extensive review on a number of different strollers, including which ones are better for jogging or which ones are better for navigating the urban sprawl. If you want personalized service, you can check out Strollerqueen's Website at www.strollerqueen.com. She offers a consultation service for a $30 fee giving you the best stroller for your needs, including the best deal you can get for it.

43| Stroller Accessories In Any Kind Of Weather

When traveling, it's always a good idea to find out about the climate and weather conditions of your destination ahead of time. That way, you can be prepared to dress both you and baby appropriately for the trip. If you're bringing a stroller, keep in mind that with a few accessories, you can protect your infant from many of the elements. Some strollers come with these accessories, but if yours doesn't, you can always find them at a stroller specialty shop or one of the major infant retailers, like Babies R Us.

Foot Muff – Many of the better stroller lines come with these, but if yours doesn't, you can always purchase one separately. Ideal for cold weather days, the boot cover attaches through the harness of your stroller and wraps around your baby or toddler for warmth. JJ Coles makes a version for infants as well as toddlers that fit most types of strollers.

Rain Cover – If a rain cover comes with your stroller, you'll likely snap it on for a custom fit. It provides a clear vinyl shade to keep the rain out, but lets baby enjoy the view. If you need to purchase it separately, you can get a one-size-fits-most version, which rests on top of your stroller. Especially For Baby at Babies R Us makes stroller rain covers.

Sun Shade – These might snap on to your stroller much like a rain cover does if your stroller comes with it. The best ones are UV-filtered to keep the sun's harmful rays away from your child. They're typically made of a soft woven fabric that drapes over your stroller and allows your infant to see out.

Sun Canopy – Just about every stroller has a sun canopy with the exception of some of the most basic umbrella strollers. However, if you've ever toyed with one of these, you know it takes some adjustment throughout your walk to keep the sun out. Short of using a blanket to cover baby up, you can purchase a canopy attachment that'll block out much more sunlight than a standard stroller canopy will. *Protect A Bub* makes a canopy shade attachment that maintains visibility for your child while providing sun protection.

Mosquito Net – If you're going somewhere tropical where mosquitoes are abound, this is one handy stroller accessory to have. It's typically a mesh fabric which attaches snugly to your stroller via an elasticized bottom. They're much more common on European models of strollers, but you can purchase them separately. See if your stroller manufacturer carries them. If not, baby retailers or places selling outdoor gear do carry them.

44| Stroller Accessories To Keep You Organized

When you're on the go with your stroller, it's always nice to have somewhere to stash your stuff in a convenient, organized place. This is especially true if you're sprinting through the airport with your toddler to get to the gate; you'll want to have all your documents on hand when you get there. If you're looking for stroller accessories that'll keep you from juggling a drink in your hand and travel documents in the other, try one of these nifty organizational accessories for your stroller.

Carry You Milan Deluxe Stroller Organizer ($40) – Carry You makes a line of practical bags for the stroller, including cup holders, saddle bags, and organizers. The Deluxe Stroller Organizer accommodates two cups – a sippy for your tot and a drink for you. But it also provides a large mesh bag and smaller organizers for papers, keys, small toys, and any other loose item you need to store. It attaches to the back of your stroller and is constructed of a nylon mesh material. It works nicely for travel because it packs flat and will collapse with your stroller as well.

Skip Hop Dash – Skip Hop makes organizational tools for the modern parent, from a sculptural bottle drying rack to diaper bags that do double-duty as stroller bags. We like the Dash because it looks deceptively like a messenger bag, yet it attaches to the rear of your stroller with its own stroller straps. Plus it's the ideal size for boarding on a plane, but has enough room for all your essentials. It has a total of 10 pockets to keep you organized as well as convenient outside pockets that'll fit baby's bottle.

45| Stroller Wheel Maintenance

If you're taking your stroller on a trip, likely you'll encounter a lot of terrain with it from airport floor tiles to urban sidewalks. In most instances, you'll find that your stroller won't need any special care or maintenance. However, there are a few things you can do to keep your stroller in top shape, compliments of Strollerqueen, Janet McLaughlin.

- Every 6-8 weeks, lubricate the wheels of your stroller. Different manufacturers have different suggestions. Peg Perego recommends you use Pledge furniture polish.

- For general cleaning, if you have a stroller with quick-release wheels, you can simply pop them off, scrub them with a brush, and rinse them in the sink.

- Every time your stroller goes in the sand, you should clean them off. All you have to do is hose the wheels and dry them off.

46| How To Protect Your Stroller During Plane Travel

Just because there's the possibility that your stroller could get damaged doesn't mean you have to shy away completely from bringing it with you on a flight. If you're going to fly with a stroller and check it at the gate, there are steps you can take to help ensure its safety. And if you are going to bring a stroller, your best bet is to bring one that folds flat without much effort. The last thing you want is to be stuck struggling to collapse your stroller during the last call for boarding.

With that in mind, here are a few words of wisdom we garnered from the Strollerqueen, Janet McLaughlin.

- Take a stroller with you to the airport that latches to stay shut. One way to ensure that your stroller stays folded is to use a luggage strap and wrap it around your stroller before you check it in at the gate.

- Although a stroller bag is one way to protect your stroller, parents should keep this in mind: some airlines don't like the use of a bag because they don't know what's in it. Also, stroller bags that are made of canvas will protect from scratches, but not a drop from the cargo hold onto the tarmac.

- Some people have gotten around the problem of the stroller bag by wrapping their strollers in bubble wrap and adding "fragile" stickers throughout. You've got an instant affordable means of protection and airport personnel will feel more assured knowing what's underneath the packaging. Plus, baggage handlers who know it's indeed a stroller underneath the wrap may handle the item with more care.

Helpful Hint: One way around the stroller dilemma is to use a car seat attachment like the one by GoGo Babyz or the car seat stroller by Sit N Stroll by Triple Play Products.

47| What Airline Travel Can Do To Your Stroller

Taking a stroller with you on plane travel can mean risky business for parents. Though we'd like to tell you that the airport baggage handlers treat all of your luggage with kid gloves – including your stroller – we hear it isn't so. We caught up with Strollerqueen Janet McLaughlin, the guru of strollers, to find out the inside story.

According to Strollerqueen, there is an ongoing problem with airlines trashing strollers in the last few years. This is due in part to the fact that in recent years, airlines have experienced a significant drop in profits. In order to cut costs, one of the things they've done is contract out baggage handlers who aren't necessarily as careful when they handle luggage. People who have complained haven't necessarily found the airlines to be helpful in responding to a damaged stroller, either. If you read a typical airline baggage policy, fragile items are not covered. Many airlines consider a stroller a fragile item.

The lesson here? Parents beware if you're planning to check your strollers at the gate. Think twice about packing your most expensive brand new stroller on the trip. Or at least take steps to protect it.

48| Four Nifty Products For Traveling With Baby

Gadgets are well-designed, used for everyday tasks, and take a new spin on an existing concept. Here are just a few gadgets you might want to try out for your next trip with baby:

Zuca ($130-145)-- Ever use your luggage as a seat? Ever want to use your luggage as a seat, but just couldn't wing it? This wheeled luggage functions as a seat as well as carry-all for your travel gear.

Teeny Towels ($8 for four-pack)-- If you ever worried about having room to stock towels for wiping your child's hands clean, worry no more. These teeny towels do really come in a petite package - a keychain dispenser that can attach to your diaper bag or stroller.

Teeny Pads ($7)-- For travel and on the go, we like products that pack small. Teeny pads is actually a diaper changing pad that is machine washable, packs petite, and clips onto your diaper bag or stroller.

Diaper Bridge ($40)-- When there just isn't a changing table around, this product makes up for it by attaching to a sink. It sounds odd, but if you've ever been to a restroom without a changing station and needed to change baby's diaper, you'll realize the thoughtfulness put into this product.

49| How To Avoid Diaper Disasters

Diaper changes quickly become second nature for any parent with an infant. Dealing with diaper duty on the home front is one thing, but dealing with it while you're traveling is another.

We fondly recall the story of a husband and wife who were in the midst of changing their toddler's diaper on the plane. Just when they removed one soiled diaper, their tot decided it was time to go again. It was at this time, they both discovered they were out of diapers. You can picture the rest of the scenario. Don't let this be you. Follow our advice on how to avoid diaper disasters for your next trip.

- Always have a stash of diapers in your diaper bag, so you can just grab it and go when you're heading out. Fill your diaper bag up when you get back from an outing, not when you're headed out the door. But always check before you leave your hotel, cruise ship, or whatever your temporary headquarters may be to make sure you've got enough to keep baby clean and happy.

- For a trip, pack enough diapers in your luggage to get you to your destination and then pack some more.

- If you're heading on the plane, change your baby's diapers shortly before boarding the plane or for a drive in the car.

- Many planes do have a changing table for baby in one of the lavatories. If you're not sure, inquire before you get to the airport. It might be a good idea to find out what infant supplies, if any, the airline has. Some may have disposable diapers, wipes, and creams. Don't expect that they will, but it's always good to find out before your flight.

- If there isn't a changing table on board and baby needs a diaper change, you might just have to make do with an empty seat aisle. If that isn't available, your own seat will have to do.

- Even though you're out and about and having a good time, remember to check baby's diaper often. It's better to change it when you can stop and take a break than when you realize you've got a mess to clean up.

50| Packing It Up: Diaper Bags For On The Go

Diaper bags are indispensable for day trips around town or week-long trips to the Caribbean. In general, we think that most diaper bags suitable for daily use work just fine for on the road or on the plane. But just in case, here's a little summary of what we think works best for hauling around your baby gear around on trips.

Messenger Diaper Bag: We love this because you just throw it across your shoulder and let it rest on your hip, and the bag stays put. They're easy on, easy off. With some tote bags, you might have a functional and fashionable item for your daily outings, but when you're running to the airport terminal with tot in hand, you don't want to worry about a bulky diaper bag falling off your shoulder. We like the Sherpani Lena Diaper ($60) bags for weekend trips or daily use on longer ones. They have just the right amount of style with an internal fabric print. The functionality of the bottle pockets, key fob, and a wet pocket for your diapers doesn't hurt either.

The Dad Diaper Bag: These days, dads are just as involved in a baby's care as moms. So it's only natural that there should be a diaper bag suitable for fathers to carry as well. They basically have all the same features and functionality of other diaper bags, but are designed to appeal to the fathers. Diaper Dude ($55-$60) has several messenger bags in their line that'll appeal to the urban, hip father. They also have a few bags geared specifically for moms as well.

Backpack Diaper Bag: The backpack diaper bags work equally well for walks around town as they do when you're headed out to the beach or camping.

51| Stroller Products For On The Go

Wouldn't it be great if you could purchase a stroller that would come with every single feature you could ever want and need? Since that stroller doesn't exist, we suggest you customize yours to have all the unique accessories that would make your life easier as you wheel your tot during your travels. Here are some picks:

The Stroller Stretcher ($15)– Ever try to steer a stroller with one hand through the airport while you're actually carrying your cranky toddler in the other? If you've got one designed with such superior maneuverability, you've got a great set of wheels. For those who need a little help, this attachment lets you steer with one hand with ease.

Sit N Stroll With Sunshade ($219) – OK. This one isn't exactly an accessory per se, but it is a great product for traveling that we know makes a lot of parents' lives easier. It operates as a car seat and converts to a stroller – just shove the handle and out come the retractable wheels. It's perfect for use on the airplane and then wheeling through the airport. We like the one with the sunshade, in case you're taking your little one outdoors.

Hands Free Jogging Stroller Adapter by Stroll Smart ($50)– If you jog with baby, this accessory will make your life tremendously easier. Perfect for everyday use, daytrips to the beach, or that week-long stay at the condo, the hands free running adapter attaches at your waist and lets you jog freely with your stroller. What's more, it's compact enough to pack flat in your luggage.

Baby Travel Gear For Meals

52| Disposable Mealtime Gear

When it comes to mealtime gear for your little one, you'll want products that are easily packable, portable, and cleanable. We found a few items that are disposable as well, making your travels just that much lighter.

First Years Take and Toss Spill-proof Cups ($15 for 24-pack): We like these because you can put them in the dishwasher and use them again, but they're meant for temporary use. At less than 70 cents a cup, you can take a few along for the journey, toss them when you're done, and save the rest for the next vacation. You can also get take and toss snack containers as well as a flatware set, which includes disposable spoons and forks.

Topper to Go ($20 for four kits): The box comes in a four pack and includes a mat and disposable bib, sippy cup, fork, and spoon. We like the idea for its convenience; everything's packed in the cup, so you just grab it and go.

Pampers Pocket Bibsters ($23 for 128-count in size large): These disposable bibs catch the food nicely and keep liquids off infant clothes with a leak-proof liner.

Formula One Shot Bags ($14 for 100): It's an easy way to store formula servings for your infant during travel, and comes with a funnel tip for easy pouring. Divvy up the portions before you go on your trip and when it comes to making baby's bottle there's less fuss and less mess.

53| Breastfeeding And Travel

If you're a breastfeeding mom and your infant isn't yet at the solid feeding stage, you do have a simpler task of feeding baby. However, we know that breastfeeding, especially when traveling, does present its own set of challenges. So here are our suggestions for breastfeeding while traveling.

- Consider carrying your baby in a pouch or sling, which helps to facilitate easier breastfeeding, especially when you're on the move.

- Dress in clothing that makes it easier to breastfeed discreetly. Wear a nursing tank under a loose blouse. Get a few tops designed just for nursing. Or consider throwing on a shawl or a blanket over your shoulder.

- On the plane, take a seat by the window. If you're traveling with your spouse, use him as your buffer to the rest of the plane. It's helpful to nurse an infant during take-off and landings to ease the discomfort due to change in air pressure.

- When you're out and about, look for the women's lounges in department stores, dressing rooms in boutiques, baby centers at amusement parks, family centers at airports, and quiet benches at the park. Your own car is a great way to nurse in semi-private. Remember, there are times when there really is no private place to nurse, so you'll just have to make do with some discretion and perhaps a blanket.

- Remember that breastfeeding your child is a positive and natural way to bond and provide nourishment for your baby. A woman in the U.S. has a constitutional right to breastfeed her child in any location she can go to legally. If you have concerns about laws regarding breastfeeding in your state, you can refer to the La Leche League Website (www.lalecheleague.com), which provides comprehensive legislative information on breastfeeding in each state across the U.S.

- If you're in a foreign country, try doing some research ahead of time on the customs and laws on public breastfeeding. Try observing the local culture to see what's acceptable and what's not in terms of breastfeeding.

54| Meals In The Car

Feeding baby in the car can be simple enough as long as you're prepared. For easy mealtimes with baby in the car, here are some quick tips:

- If both Mom and Dad are traveling in the car, have one person drive and have the other person sit in the back to attend to baby's needs.

- Pack a cooler with all the food and drink essentials you need for the trip. Have them on hand and within easy reach.

- For bottles that need warming, you can bring a portable bottle warmer that works on its own or plugs into your cigarette lighter.

- Have plastic bags on hand for tossing out trash and large Ziploc bags for storing baby's bottle. Bring two sets of bottles so you can use one while the other is being cleaned.

- Store baby food in easy to use containers. Baby food is contaminated once you dip a used spoon back into the jar. Rather than tossing out food or dealing with storage, take your baby food out ahead of time and pack them into one ounce individual food containers that you can toss into a large Ziploc bag.

- If you're just driving off somewhere and baby isn't tired yet, go ahead and feed her a meal or her bottle. If you've been on the road for a while and she's hungry, pull over and feed her.

- Use disposable bibs. They keep messes at bay and they pack up nicely. Use them again if you want to wipe baby clean, or toss it out and grab a fresh one.

55| Mealtime On Planes

Feeding baby on the plane doesn't have to be a complex task, but it does require a little bit of planning. Gone are the days of travel when you could just pick up and go – then stop somewhere to eat when it suits you.

We want feeding baby on the go to be as simple as possible for the traveling parent, so we've put together our best plane tips from parents who've flown the friendly, and not-so-friendly, skies.

- When you book your flight, contact the airline to reserve a kid's meal for toddlers or request an infant meal for babies. Not all airlines carry them, but most longer flights and international flights with major airlines do have baby food. Ask what amenities they have for your infant at this time so you'll know what to expect.

- Regardless of whether an airline carries food for an infant, you'll want to pack your own. You don't want to have to rely on their service to feed your little one if she's hungry. Pack everything in sealed plastic bags and plastic containers.

- If you're planning on bringing a bottle, you should be able to get it heated on the plane. This is another thing you should check ahead of time if you're concerned about it.

- Pack a stash of disposable bibs. They fold flat, you can use them more than once if you want to wipe them clean, and they're convenient to just toss when you're done.

- Have a hand sanitizer on hand to clean your hands and baby's. They come in travel sizes and are really portable.

- Wipes for cleaning up messes during and after eating are invaluable. For travel, get a handy travel size pack.

- If your infant is on solids, you can feed her in her seat or on your lap. Use your best judgment as to what's easier and safer. If there's turbulence, you'll want to leave her in her seat.

- You'll be able to use disposable utensils from the plane, but for younger infants, bring your own. Coated spoons will be more suitable for sensitive gums.

56| Six Ways To Make Dining Out With Baby Successful

Let's face it. Dining out with an infant certainly isn't the same as having a meal out when there were only two of you. However, you can dine out and enjoy your meal, too. You'll have to multi-task, but with these tips you're sure to handle the night with ease:

1. Arrive early. There's nothing that will spoil an outing with baby at a restaurant than arriving to discover you have an hour to wait and the restaurant is so packed you can only expect service won't be much more prompt. Avoiding the crowds by dining early will give you more flexibility to juggle eating your own meal and attend to baby – without dealing with a long wait.

2. Pick an appropriate restaurant. There are some places that are more appropriate to take your baby to when eating out. Pick a restaurant with a casual atmosphere and enough bustle to create a moderate noise level. You don't want your toddler's whining or the baby's crying to be the silence breaker in a restaurant.

3. Choose your seating wisely. A booth may be a more convenient, self-contained area to lay out baby's gear and have your meal. For breastfeeding moms, a booth can offer more privacy. A patio seat can provide enough action to keep a toddler distracted and allow you to dine on your meal.

4. Pitch in your efforts. If both you and your spouse are dining with baby together, switch off and let one person eat while the other person attends to baby.

5. Keep it short. When you're eating out with a little one, you might not have time to stay a leisurely three hours at your meal. Expect to order your food and eat it quickly. If your child is doing well, then consider staying a bit longer to enjoy the time out.

6. Be prepared to leave. Sometimes a crying baby or cranky toddler just isn't up for a meal on the town. Have your belongings ready for a quick exit should you need to pay the bill and go in a hurry.

Baby Travel Gear for Sleeping

57| Six Ways To Make The Most Of Baby's Nap Time

Traveling with baby has its own challenges. Between planning for naps, feedings, diaper changes, playtime, and quiet time, one wonders how there is any time left in the day. However, though it is always a good idea to take baby's routines into consideration, there's no reason why you can't let baby nap and spend some time enjoying your vacation as well. Here are six ways to do just that.

1. Hire a sitter and spend the afternoon exploring the town while baby gets naptime and playtime at the hotel.

2. Switch off with your spouse throughout the vacation. One day, Dad gets to go out golfing while Mom relaxes on the hotel deck with a book. One day, Mom gets to go out for a spa afternoon, while Dad catches up on the TV news at the hotel room – with headphones.

3. Take baby out for a jog in the stroller. Then relax and enjoy the waves while she snoozes.

4. Go for a hike and put baby in the backpack carrier. Enjoy the scenery while she peacefully drifts off for a nap.

5. Take a well-timed drive out to enjoy the landscape just before your little one's nap. By the time you come back, she'll be ready to join you on your next excursion.

6. Spend a few hours at the beach relaxing with drinks and some munchies. Put baby down for a nap in the shade while you and hubby enjoy a seashore picnic.

58| Helping Baby Adjust To Time Zone Changes

If you're taking your infant with you across multiple time zones, you may need to help her adjust to a new schedule. Babies are adaptable, but like adults, need some time to adjust to new surroundings and changes. The best way to handle time zone changes is to start preparing for your adjustment before you arrive at your destination.

- Try planning a flight that would work best with your infant's schedule. Depending on how far you're going and your baby's temperament, this might be a red-eye flight or it might be an afternoon flight. Use your best judgment.

- You can start by making adjustments to your baby's bedtime a few days before the trip in 20-minute increments. Move her bedtime earlier or later, depending on the time difference at your arrival destination.

- If you're flying on a plane, make the mental adjustment to function on the new time zone as soon as you depart. The best way to do this is by changing your watch to accommodate the time of your destination.

- When you arrive, try putting your infant to bed according to the current time zone.

- During the daytime, allow lots of time outdoors as this helps the body adjust to the current environment.

- Be flexible with activities during the first few days and accommodate baby's need for an adjustment period. Everyone on the trip will be much happier in the long run. Remember, adults can take three days to adjust to a time zone, so be sensitive to your baby's routine.

59| Sleep Tight Tips For Little Ones

If you're traveling for the first time with an infant or going to an unfamiliar location, you might be worried about whether your little one will sleep well during the trip.

One mother put it aptly when she said, "Babies will tend to get the sleep they need one way or another. The same can't be said for parents." However, there are some things you can do to ensure your little one will get her much needed rest – so you can get yours, too.

- Establish a familiar routine. Now when we say routine, we don't mean a rigid schedule by the clock. Instead, keep the general rhythms that you do when you're at home. For some parents this may mean a very loose approach where baby adapts to the parent's routine. For others, this may mean that Mom and Dad plan their trip around baby's nap and feeding times.

- Bring familiar items to help your infant adjust. This could be her much needed pacifier, a familiar blanket, or a toy from home.

- At bedtimes, use the same routine you do at home. If you give your baby a bath, change the baby into sleepwear, and then put your baby to sleep, follow the same pattern. Babies will do well with familiar rhythms.

- For naps, have a stroller on hand if your baby sleeps in the stroller. Use a baby carrier if your baby will sleep in that. Either way, both are useful for getting out and about during naptimes.
- Create a dim place for baby's sleep time. This may just mean turning out the lights at the hotel in the evening once your baby goes to sleep. One parent we know solved the dilemma of being able to keep the light on for her and her spouse by opening up the closet, moving in the portable crib, and suspending a sheet from the top of the closet over the portable crib. It became an instant private, darkened area. If you decide to try this, make sure the sheet is secure and that baby can't pull it down.

60| Sleeping At The Hotel

Sleep time for infants can be a prime time for parents during traveling. Catch up on your own much needed rest, pick up a book, or switch off with your spouse or another adult so one person can watch the baby while the other heads out. If you're planning your trip and wondering just what you should bring with you, find out what you really need and don't need to bring. Many hotels do carry *Pack N Plays* or similar portable cribs. If you don't want to lug your own, call the hotel ahead of time and see if they can supply you with what you need. One cautionary note: make sure the equipment is safe and in good condition.

In 2000, the Consumer Product Safety Commission found 80% of the hotels reviewed had unsafe cribs. However, since that time, a program has been in place to promote a safety initiative to ensure that cribs are safe. The CPSC recommends parents find out whether a hotel has guidelines to make sure their hotel cribs are safe. If your toddler has graduated to the big bed and you have room in the car, try adding a bedrail to make sleep time safer. First Years carries a single bed rail with a mesh screen. It's relatively easy to secure to the underside of a mattress.

Helpful Hint: Don't forget, if you don't want to bring bulky infant gear with you, there are baby equipment rental facilities that can accommodate your needs for portable cribs, bed rails, and other items.

61| Sleeping: The Plane and Car

One good thing about sleeping on the move with your little one is that sleep and movement go together at this age. Many parents find infants and toddlers will be lulled to sleep in the car, or will fall asleep in Mom or Dad's arms during a walk, if it's anywhere near their naptimes. If you're wondering just how your infant or toddler should be sleeping while you're headed to your vacation destination, here's what you can expect.

On the plane: If you're on a red eye flight going across the coast or going on a transatlantic journey, you'll likely need to figure out sleeping accommodations. Since fares for children under 2 may be reduced, do consider getting your infant her own seat. If you have a young infant, consider reserving your seats in the bulkhead section. Check with your airline first, but most supply a bassinet for you that attaches to the wall. Also check the height and size restrictions, as some bassinet sizes vary. During an especially turbulent flight, you'll likely want to strap your infant into her own child seat. Toddlers should have their own child seat as well. If a flight is empty, you might be able to snag an extra seat in your row so your toddler can spread out during sleep time. As with any flight, if you encounter turbulence, have your toddler in her own seat.

In the car: If your car is moving, your infant or toddler should be strapped in her car seat at all times. If you plan on being on the road while your little one needs rest, she should always be sleeping in her car seat. Never give in to the temptation to hold your baby while she's sleeping in the car.

62| Do It Yourself Hotel Baby Proofing

Maybe you've got your own whole house full of childproof locks, baby gates, and outlet covers. But when you're traveling to new places, you won't have the same set-up. However, you might not have to do as much work as you think. Try these simple steps to baby proofing your hotel accommodations.

1. Call the hotel you're staying at and ask what sort of baby proofing equipment, if any, they have. If the hotel does offer the service, request to have your room baby proofed in advance of your stay.

2. Assess what additional items you might need to bring. Possible baby proofing items include outlet covers, faucet covers, toilet latches, and bi-fold locks if the closet opens as a bi-fold. An inexpensive way to childproof is to use pipe cleaners to secure items like drapery cords and masking tape to cover items like electrical sockets.

3. When you get to the hotel, take a few minutes to do an inspection. Check the cabinets for any hazardous objects that may be accessible to your child. Get down low and look for small objects that may be choking hazards.

Helpful Hint: For some locations that are child safety approved, look at Safe Stay's Website at www.asafestay.com. They list additional suggestions on what safety hazards to look out for as well as child-safe hotels in major cities across the United States.

63| Create Your Own Travel First Aid Kit

Whether you're traveling on a weekend road trip out of town or taking a plane to an exotic locale, have a travel first aid kit on hand you can throw in your suitcase. A first aid kit should have all the basics you need in a pinch, should you need to deal with mishaps or illness. It's always better to be prepared than to scramble around for the things you need if your child falls ill or needs medical attention.

Our suggestion? Package everything up in a child's lunch box – it's fun, easy to spot, and completely self-contained. Get trial sizes whenever you can to eliminate bulk. Here's a list of the basics for your travel first aid kit:

- First aid guide – Get one geared towards children and infants.

- Medical prescriptions - If your baby has any prescriptions, make sure you pack them. Also, include your doctor's phone number and an oral syringe to administer the medicine.

- Thermometer - If your infant gets a fever, you'll want to be able to check as soon as possible to ensure the right medication is administered.

- Antibiotic ointment – It'll help heal cuts and scrapes as well as stave off infection.

- Liquid soap- Use this tidy package to clean up cuts and scrapes, as well as any baby mishaps.

- Sterile bandages – Use them to stop bleeding from little cuts and scrapes. Petite round or oval shapes are perfect for infants.

- Infant acetaminophen - Use Children's Tylenol or the equivalent. Use this for relieving fevers as well as aches and pains from teething, colds, flu, or chicken pox.

- Gas Reliever – Pack Baby Mylicon or its generic equivalent. If your infant has gas pains, this will help relieve it.

- Pedialyte - If your infant has diarrhea or dehydration, you'll want to replenish her fluids.

Helpful Hint #1: You can buy well-known brands like Tylenol or Mylicon, but if you want to save a bit of cash, go to your pharmacy and get the generic equivalent.

Helpful Hint #2: To save space, buy a box of Pedialyte freezer pops. They don't come frozen, so you can pack a few 2.1 oz. packages into your first aid kit.

64| Be Prepared: The Travel Emergency Checklist

You're blissfully dreaming of taking a break from the daily doldrums of cleaning spit-up from the highchair, and sailing to warmer waters on the long awaited cruise. But wait. Before you start packing your bags, make sure you have your emergency checklist updated.

In a true emergency, you won't want to spend precious time locating essential information. Here's an emergency checklist to keep things calm:

Emergency numbers: Create a list of emergency contacts. This includes your family doctor and medical contacts while away from home.

Insurance information: Have a record of your insurance carrier, medical record number, and insurance contact information. It's also a good idea to find out what you're covered for and where if you're outside of your local coverage area.

Prescriptions: Make sure you have enough to last throughout the trip or a feasible plan to get more medication if you need it.

Baby Proofing: Whether you're actually embarking on a cruise or braving the outdoors, check the accommodations at your destination ahead of time. Think about what items you need to bring to baby proof your stay.

Immunizations: Check with your public health authorities on recommended immunizations if you're traveling abroad. Find out if any vaccines are appropriate for you or your infant.

Helpful Hint: Don't forget to include emergency contact information for mom, dad and siblings as well. Parents need to be in good health too! You can create a laminated reference card with emergency numbers and your insurance information as well, including your medical record number and contact information. Pack the reference card in your travel first aid kit and then keep a second set of information with you. For your spare set of emergency information, you can make a separate card or put everything on your PDA.

65| Resources For Travel Safety

You've got good intentions. You mean to make travel as safe as possible, but you're really not sure where to look. Well, we've got that covered for you. Whether you need information on health concerns, first aid, or international travel, these resources are all great places to find out about travel safety.

Centers for Disease Control and Prevention: Find out everything from how long you can store breast milk to how you can prevent diarrhea in young children and infants. Worried about health issues relating to a specific destination? You can find that here as well.

Transportation Security Administration: For information on getting through the screening process, what you can and can't bring on the plane, as well as information specific to packing baby food, formula, and breast milk, check out the Transportation Security Administration Website.

U.S. Consular Affairs: If you're concerned about travel safety abroad, legal issues pertaining to traveling out of the country with children, finding American doctors in a foreign country, or figuring out who to contact in the event of an emergency, you can find all of the information here.

American Academy of Pediatrics– The American Academy of Pediatrics issues guidelines on car seat safety, plane travel, and sun protection. We've included a few links that you'll find useful for home and during your travels.

- Car Seats:
  http://www.aap.org/family/carseatguide

- Sun Protection:
  http://www.aap.org/sections/media/SunSafety

- Vaccinations:
  http://www.aap.org/healthtopics/immunizations

- Safety and First Aid Checklist:
  http://www.aap.org/healthtopics/safety

66| Road Trip Safety Rules

It's a done deal. You've made the decision to make the six-hour drive across two state lines to get to Grandma's house for the holidays. Getting there with calm nerves is one thing, but getting there safely is another. We've put together some road trip safety rules for traveling with baby.

Rule #1 – Always put your infant in a child safety seat in the backseat. According to the National Highway Traffic Safety Administration (NHTSA), it's the safest place.

Rule #2 – Keep your infant in a rear-facing infant car seat or convertible until he or she is at least 20 pounds and one year old. After one year and after your baby hits the 20 pound marker, you can use a forward facing convertible car seat.

Rule #3 – If you have a two-seater car – take heed: the force of an airbag can cause serious injuries or kill children and infants. If you do have the option to turn your airbag off in the passenger seat where your infant will be, do so. It's the safest alternative to suffering the extreme force of an airbag, should it deploy.

Rule #4 – Never, ever take your child out of her car seat while driving. Infants and young children may cry and scream while you're driving. Do not remove your child from the one piece of protection that could save his or her life should you get into a car crash. If she's tired, likely she'll fall asleep in the next several minutes. If she's hungry, pull the car over and feed her. At the risk or repeating ourselves, whatever the problem, you can always stop the car at a safe location and attend to your little one.

Rule #5 – Before you hit the road, remember to check that the car seat is attached properly to the car and that your child is harnessed in securely. Remember these rules of thumb:

- A secure car seat should not move more than one inch in either direction.

- If your car seat has a tether and your car can accommodate it, use it. It'll restrict the forward motion of the car seat in the event of a crash.

- Make sure your infant is buckled securely. The harness should be snug, but not binding.

Helpful Hint: If you have any questions about the installation of your car seat, you can check with an organization like the NHTSA. Their Website at www.nhtsa.dot.gov has a list of places you can bring your car to check for proper installation.

67| Safety And Plane Travel

Many parents decide to travel to their destination by plane. Some infants and toddlers just can't handle the long car rides, and the travel itinerary includes faraway places. If you'll be doing some plane travel with your infant in tow, there are some safety measures you can take.

- The Federal Aviation Administration (FAA) says the safest place on the plane for baby is in her own seat in an approved restraint system. This is especially true during heavy flight turbulence.

- If you do decide to buy your child a seat, remember that the FAA requires car seats to be attached at a window seat. Remember that your seat will likely be in the middle.

- Most U.S. made car seats have FAA approval for use on airplanes. If you want to double-check, it should say, "FAA Approved in Accordance with 14CFR 21.305(d), Approved for Aircraft Use Only". Foreign made seats must have a stamp of approval from their government or the United Nations. However, it's always a good idea to double-check with the airline as car seats wider than 16" across may not fit on an airplane seat.

- An alternative to the infant car seat is the first harness child safety device approved by the FAA in 2006 for use on airplanes only. *The Cares Device*, by AmSafe Aviation, is a shoulder harness and belt for children 22 pounds to 44 pounds in weight, so it's appropriate for most older infants, toddlers, and young children.

68| To Your Health - And Baby's

Traveling with an infant or toddler means you'll be encountering a great deal of environmental changes and possible travel-related risks. However, if you take the right precautions, there's no reason why your journey shouldn't be injury and illness free. We've gathered some advice on keeping you and your baby healthy.

· The top reported childhood health problems due to travel, according to the Centers for Disease Control and Prevention (CDC), is diarrhea, malaria, and accidents due to motor vehicles and water. For those visiting third world countries, children are at the risk of contracting malaria or tuberculosis.

· If your infant is breastfeeding, you have a built-in solution for preventing illnesses from food and water. Diarrhea can be contracted through a contaminated water source.

· If you're traveling in a country where the water supply is questionable, your best bet is to use purified or bottled water to wash your hands, brush your teeth, and prepare infant foods and formula. Remember to avoid ice cubes if you're not sure about the water source.

- Malaria is a disease transmitted by female Anopheles mosquitoes and occurs mostly in tropical and subtropical areas. Africa, Asia, Central America, and South America have statistically harbored more cases of malaria transmission, according to the CDC. Using mosquito nets, staying in screened areas, and using mosquito coils are effective at keeping mosquitoes at bay. If you decide to use DEET products, the American Academy of Pediatrics (AAP) deems products with up to 30% DEET safe for infants over two months of age. A 50% concentration of DEET is deemed safe for adults. For more information on prevention and treatment, consult the CDC Website (www.cdc.gov) or your health care provider.

- The top cause of death in children who travel is the car accident. We can't stress enough the importance of child safety seats. For more information on how to keep your child safe, refer to our tip, "Road Trip Safety Rules".

- The second cause of death in children who travel is drowning. While we certainly don't want to be morbid here, we do want to make you aware of the dangers. When you're traveling, follow all the same precautions you would at home. Never leave an infant or young child unsupervised around water – even if it's only two inches deep.

Helpful Hint: Mosquitoes feed mainly between dusk and dawn, so extra care should be taken during these hours to avoid contact.

69| Childcare and Travel: How To Assess What's Best

It's not always easy leaving your infant in the care of someone else. Especially when you're traveling, you want to make sure you're leaving your baby in the best hands. Childcare can come in the form of agency supplied nannies, baby-sitters for hire, or childcare programs at resorts and hotels. If you have a nanny you can bring along on your trip, great.

But for everyone else who needs childcare, we've put together some things you should consider when contemplating childcare away from home.

- Make sure you have childcare in place long before you reach your destination and make a confirmation before you arrive.

- Do the background research on the nanny, babysitter, or agency you're using ahead of time. Ask family and friends for recommendations. Try online parent boards.

- If you are hiring an individual, make sure you speak to her ahead of time and get references. If it's an agency or childcare program, interview the director.

- If you're hiring a nanny or babysitter, ask if she is CPR certified, how much experience she has, what ages she's worked with, and whether you feel she'll be a good fit for your infant. Never discount your gut feeling.

- If you're working with a childcare program, you also need to find out the ratio of childcare providers to children, what necessities do they provide, what activities are included, and what hours they're available.

- Last, but not least, find out what you'll be paying and establish a set number of hours.

70| Traveling Abroad: Passport Requirements

Paperwork, though perhaps one of the least desirable parts of travel planning, is a necessary part of your travel plans. The requirements for traveling abroad are changing. If you're planning on travel outside of the United States, you should be aware of the documents you need to take with you. If you're planning any travel outside of the United States, you should get a passport for each member of the family. This includes baby, parents, and other children.

As of January 23, 2007, you now need a passport if you're planning on flying from the U.S. to Canada, Mexico, Central America, South America, the Caribbean, and Bermuda. Starting January 1, 2008, passport requirements may also include car travel and cruise travel outside of the U.S. to places like Mexico, Canada, and the Caribbean. If you're a parent traveling on your own, keep in mind you'll need to have additional documentation on hand when traveling abroad; regardless of whether you're married, separated, or divorced. For any travel outside of the U.S., many countries require a notarized Permission to Travel letter. In some instances, proof of custody is a requirement as well.

Helpful Hint: You don't have to create your own Permission to Travel Letter. The Family Travel Forum Website has one available for you, and you can download it directly from their website at www.familytravelforum.com

71| Getting A Passport For You And Baby

If you already have a U.S. passport for you and baby, good for you! You're ready to travel. If not, have no worries. We'll explain the process for you.

First off, whether the passport is for you or for your child, you do have to appear in a person to apply. However, the process can be easier if you start preparing your materials before you visit a passport agency. You also should apply for a passport several months before you travel.

It typically takes six weeks after processing the application for you to get your passport. Here's a step-by-step process for getting a passport for you or baby.

1. First, get a passport application. An easy way to do this is download it off the Bureau of Consular Affairs Website at www.travel.state.gov. You can also find passport applications at certain post offices as well.

2. Fill out the application and make an appointment to go to an approved passport acceptance facility. They have thousands of locations, so you don't have to worry about finding one within reasonable distance to you. The Consular Affairs Website maintains a list so you'll know where to go.

3. Gather all the necessary supporting documents. You need to provide one proof of U.S. citizenship and one proof of identity. Proof of citizenship can be an older passport or birth certificate. Proof of identity can also include an older passport or naturalization certificate or driver's license. For your little one, parent identification would be required and parent consent may be requested as well.

4. You also need to provide 2- 2"x2" photos. If you take your own, they must be taken with a frontal facial view. The image from the bottom of your chin to the top of your head should measure 1 to 1-3/8". Have a white or off-white background behind you, dress in plain clothes, and don't wear any hats or dark glasses. Prescription glasses are fine. You can also have passport photos taken at a number of photo processing locations.

5. When you go in, have your application, supporting documents, and photos on hand. Be prepared to pay the fee with a credit card, debit card, or check.

Helpful Hint: If you absolutely must get your passport sooner, you can expedite the process by paying an additional fee to get your passport in two weeks instead of six.

72| Five Signs A Toy Isn't Travel Friendly

Your child has a favorite toy, but the thought of carrying it around with you from the airport, onto the plane, into the rental car, and through the hotel, doesn't make you jump for joy. Some toys are great for entertaining little ones at home, but just won't cut it on vacation. If you're on the fence about whether or not to take a toy with you, here are five signs to help you determine if a toy is **not** travel friendly.

1. There are more than a dozen different separate parts to this toy. If the toy has multiple pieces that can get misplaced or is otherwise hard to keep track of, don't bring this toy with you on the trip.

2. You're having a hard time deciding whether to pack the toy in your luggage or take out half your wardrobe. It the toy is too bulky, heavy, or cumbersome, it's not a travel toy.

3. The toy costs more than the price of your child's reduced fare ticket. We're not sure what toy you decided to buy your youngster that carries a steep price tag, but unless you can afford to replace it without much financial concern, we recommend you don't take the toy on your trip.

4. A puncture or breakage in the toy will cause a mini flash flood in your luggage. If you have a toy that could break and subsequently drown your clothing and belongings, it's best to leave it at home.

5. Your toddler loves the toy, but the repetitive flashing lights and musical tunes of the toy will make for a very long trip… for you and the other people around you. Need we say more?

73| How To Keep Track Of Your Toddler When Traveling

If you have an active toddler and you're going on a trip, he'll probably want to spend some time on his feet running around and exploring his new environment. While this may help burn off some active toddler steam, it does present the dilemma of keeping track of a young child. And as you know, a toddler can fall out of your sight very quickly. If you have some concerns about keeping track of your toddler, here are a few ways to ensure a safe and sound environment while traveling.

- Dress up your child in bright colored shirts. Orange or reds are good, but use whatever color your fashion sense permits so long as it lets you spot your little one in an instant.

- Get a leash. We know how this sounds, and before you imagine your toddler in shackles, check out a product from Eddie Bauer called *Harness Buddy* ($10 and up). Your toddler wears a harness on his body, but it's dressed up by an adorable plush animal. If you want your harness to double as a backpack, get the *Harness Buddy* with the monkey motif.

- Get a child locator. You can find some effective, inexpensive gadgets that your toddler will be delighted to wear. *Giggle Bug* ($20) makes a child locator that comes in brightly colored ladybug shapes. Clip one on your toddler and keep the hand held activator with you. You'll be able to locate your child by following a high decibel beep as long as he's within 150 feet of you.

74| Infant Toy Safety

During your travels, you're likely to peruse through tourist shops, street vendors, or maybe even a toy store or two. Getting swept up in buying cute little trinkets for your infant or toddler can be especially tempting. However, keep in mind that not all items, no matter how cute, clever, or well designed they appear to be, are safe and appropriate for young children. Keep these infant toy safety tips in mind on your travel shopping sprees.

- Check to see if a toy has a label for age appropriateness. Though it may be tempting to purchase that trendy cool gadget for your infant, think twice. Some of these toys have small parts that can become choking hazards for your infant or small child.

- Another choking hazard is small rubber balls that are less than 1-3/4" in diameter. In general, anything that can fit through the inside of a toilet paper roll can be considered a choking hazard.

- If you're buying a plush toy, avoid anything with parts that may come loose, like glued on eyes and noses.

- Avoid plush toys that may have pellet sized stuffing. If the toy tears or breaks, these pellets can become choking hazards for young children.

75| Safety And Car Seat Toys

Car seat toys are great for entertaining babies. Whether you're going on a road trip or driving across town, it's great to have something on hand to keep your infant's interest. Toy bars, mini-mobiles, and clip-on toys are all great ideas to keep your infant occupied on the road. However, while it may be tempting to leave items like toys attached to the car seat while en route to your destination, hard objects that can come loose or projectile across the car aren't safe attached to your child's car seat. If you have any car seat toys for your baby, make sure they're secure. Otherwise, it's better to leave them off and attach them when you're out of the car or wheeling your baby around in a stroller.

One way to solve this dilemma is by picking out some soft toys you can attach to your infant's car seat. Lamaze makes a great soft *Clutch Cube* ($15) that lets little ones interact by touch, sight, sound, and smell. Your little one will love playing with the jingling chimes, exploring the peek-a-boo flaps, or smelling the cube's apple scent. It's appropriate for infants from three months to toddlers.

76| Snagging Hotel Savings

When booking hotel accommodations for your next family trip, don't get stuck paying more than you have to. There are a few ways to save money when you're booking accommodations.

1. Forget about the view - at least the ocean view. At most hotels and resorts, a garden view room is less expensive than a room with an ocean view. The standard room with a basic view is a less expensive room to book.

2. Ask for a discount. Sometimes hotels run specials or will honor discounts for card club members like AAA or American Express.

3. Check rates online as well as directly with the hotel desk. A standard room rate does not apply in the hotel world. Depending on the source you book the hotel with, you may get a different (and better) rate.

4. After you book, check back to see if there are rate changes. It's always good to book early, but you can call the hotel again to see if their rates have changed in your favor. If they have, adjust your reservation to reflect the lower rate.

77| Travel Toys For Toddlers

Toddlers are much more coordinated and love to follow the lead of adults, so toys that imitate grown-ups make good picks. During travel time, we recommend self-contained toys that you can just pack and go. We picked a few toddler-appropriate toys that would be great for travel:

Whoozit Photo Album by Manhattan Toy ($11) – We're suggesting this one because it packs flat, is nice and soft, and will keep older babies entertained long enough to buy you a few minutes of much needed peace. Plus, we think the photo album idea is great. It lets you customize with pictures and photos to keep older babies entertained. Hang onto this one through the toddler phase when your little one will be interested in finding familiar faces.

Cool Toys Box by I Play ($20) – This toy is a bit bulkier than some of the others, but completely self-contained. We think it's great for road trips, but also works for plane travel. Your toddler can play with sorted shapes and spinning gears. The hammer, power drill, and removable screws are all perfect for toddler motor skills and exploring.

78| Travel Toys From Newborn To Six Months

A child's sensory and motor skills develop rapidly during the first six months. Brightly colored objects and toys - from sounds to textured fabrics - that engage the child's various senses will be engaging and exciting for baby. If you're traveling, you'll want to bring a toy that's easily portable, rugged, and compact. There are a lot of toys to choose from, but we do have a few personal favorites that we think your little one just might enjoy.

Baby Whoozit by Manhattan Toy ($9) – We like this one because it's soft, compact (only 6" in diameter) and full of fun, colorful activities for baby to try out. Babies can make it rattle, make it squeak, bend the mouth, or enjoy their own reflection in the mirror. The best part? You can also attach it to a stroller or car seat.

Freddy The Firefly by Lamaze ($12) – This one really packs a lot of features into a tote-size toy. It's full of bright patterns that will catch a young baby's eyes. It comes in a soft package with an attached ladybug for teething, textured fabric for exploring, and wing with squeaker. The plastic hook for hanging is pretty convenient, too.

79| Travel Toys From Six Months To A Year

At this stage of the game, your baby is becoming increasingly mobile. She may go from crawling to standing between six months to a year of age. Toys that encourage movement, fine motor skills, and the exploration of cause and effect are great for babies of this age. For traveling, we've picked out a few toys that you can just pop in your diaper bag and pull out to entertain baby.

Munchkin Twisty Teether Toy ($7)– Not every toy has to be complicated. This one twists and shakes for fun sounds and comes with nubs for babies who are teething. It's also the perfect size to take on any trip.

Winkel By Manhattan Toy ($11) – This toy has a ton of bright colored, flexible rings attached to a bright polka dot square in the middle. For older babies who are teething or just like figuring out how to grasp and pull with their hands, this one is compact and easy to bring along with you.

80| Water Babies

Many vacations include ample time by the pool, ocean, or a lake. If you're bringing baby to the waterside, you'll have your own set of challenges. You can no longer cast your cares aside and jump in for a dip – at least without someone watching your little one. To make your time around the water with baby safe and fun, we've written these tips just for you.

- Safety, safety, safety. Vacations are meant for enjoyment, relaxation, and fun, but never forget to keep an eye on your little one at all times. Infants who don't have the requisite motor skills can drown in water that is less than two inches deep.

- Next on the order of business is cleanliness. If you decide to put your baby in the pool, make sure you put on the requisite swim diaper. We'll say it plainly - babies can transmit diseases to others via a parasite that is found in poop. If you're seeking a little waterproof fashion, we like *Kushies Swim Diapers* ($8) for the adorable print designs. On the other hand, if you're looking for a throwaway option, *Huggies* has disposable swim diapers for your little one.

- Now to the fun part: Toys. Water toys can add a whole other dimension of exciting play for babies. Our personal favorite is the beach ball. They come in bright colors that babies love to look at and are perfect for batting around poolside. What we like best about traveling with one is that you can deflate it and fold it flat. For a fun variation, try the *Goofy Balloonfish Beach Ball* by Intex ($4). It's a petite beach ball with fin and tail add-ons, turning it into a delightful water toy.

- Keep in mind baby's temperament and routine. If she's not enjoying the time in the water or cranky and tired, it's time to take her out and head back for a break or nap.

- Babies can get cold – fast. If the water temperature is less than 85 degrees Fahrenheit, it may be too cold. If she's shivering, take her out immediately and warm her up with a dry towel.

- It's also a good idea to dry your baby's ear out with a cotton ball or towel right after she's had a dip. Babies can get an ear infection due to water that stays trapped in their ear canals.

81| Last Minute Accommodations

Inevitably it happens. At one point or another, you're going to get stuck in a situation where you're with baby and you need to get accommodations at the last minute. There's no need to panic. Instead, some carefully placed contacts and access to the Internet should save the family from an overnight stay in the rental car.

Have a list of hotels in the local area where you're traveling. Rather than calling the toll free number, you should dial the hotel directly to inquire about accommodations. Hotel management can make a decision that could snag you a last minute room, but the customer service agent at the toll free number can't. If you make a few calls to various places and you're still out of luck, see if you can get online and book through a travel site. Places like Travelocity.com and Expedia.com get a share of the reservations available at a hotel, so you might just find an opening through an online booking agent.

Cruise Travel with Babies

82| Baby Let's Cruise

According to a 2004 article on Frommers.com, it's not uncommon for there to be 30 to 40 infants taking part in a cruise vacation. Cruises can sail for as short as three days, or extend over a period of weeks. You can also choose from destinations around the world including the Caribbean islands or countries in the Far East. Are they really great getaways for families with infants? We think so. Here's why:

- Cruising is a self-contained journey which makes it easier to access what you need to care for infants.

- You get meals, drinks, and accommodations provided for you in the price of the vacation.

- Individual and group babysitting is available on some cruise lines. You'll need to check with the cruise ship, but often babies from 6 months and up have childcare in place.

- You can do the shore excursions or not. Sometimes a stroll around the port area is fine for baby, and good for Mom and Dad.

- There are plenty of on-board activities for Mom, Dad, and kids who are at least two to three years old.

83| Best Cruise Lines For Bringing Baby On Board

Wondering what the top baby-friendly cruises are? Not all cruise ships are best for families and baby. But we've done a little research on which ones are a little more family-friendly. Here's the scoop:

- Most cruise ships have individual babysitting available, including Celebrity, Royal Caribbean, Cunard, Crystal, and Radisson Seven Seas. You'll need to check with the cruise ship, but often babies from 6 months and up have childcare in place.

- Group childcare is available with Disney, Celebrity, Carnival, Princess, and Cunard cruises.

- One thing to remember is that although babysitting may be available, activity programs start at 2 or even 3 years of age. Carnival and Norwegian are two cruise lines that have programs that start at age 2.

- Royal Caribbean has teamed up with Fisher Price toys to create a playgroup for parents and children from 6 months to three years.

- Princess Cruises has a play area that's great for tots and open to babies – parent supervision required.

- Cunard's playroom has a ball bin and doubles as a nursery.

84| Diapers And Other Cruise Pack List Essentials

Unlike a road trip, or even a plane trip, to a metropolitan vacation spot, cruising with babies presents a unique situation. Though you'll be making pit stops at ports of call, you'll be sailing through a great portion of your trip. Access to baby essentials can be rather limited, especially if you pick a destination where your ports of call consist mainly of gorgeous scenery and meandering wildlife. Besides the usual items of clothing, travel documents, and prescription medications, there are some things you don't want to assume you'll have access to. Keep in mind this pack list of baby essentials so that you're not left without the things you need.

- Baby Food – If your infant is on solids, don't expect the ship to provide this for you.
- Formula – Consider the liquid version if your baby drinks it. Otherwise you'll end up paying for pricey bottles of water to mix the formula.
- Disposable Bibs – They're so easy to pack, take up little space, and make feeding time easier.
- Diapers – Pack enough for the cruise and several days extra. Enough said.
- Diaper Wipes and Diaper Rash Cream – Bring a few travel sizes to save space.
- Large Plastic Bags – It makes disposing dirty diapers much easier and pleasant.

85| Island Hopping Hawaii Cruise

You could fly to Maui, spend a week at a vacation condo, and hang out at the beach with your infant. It's a nice, relaxing way to spend a week, but if you're keen on doing and seeing more, try flying to Hawaii for an island hop. Norwegian cruise lines has a big hold on the Hawaiian cruise market, and offers 7, 10, and 11-day vacations that allow you to explore the beauty of Hawaii - island by island. Choose from round trip cruises throughout the year from Honolulu or Maui.

One sample 7-day itinerary takes you from Maui to Honolulu, Kauai, Hilo, and Kona before returning to Maui. Moms and Dads, take your pick. You get to spend a full day at most of the ports to explore at your leisure or choose from shore excursions that allow you to enjoy Hawaii's rich culture. We think it's a great way to see more of Hawaii with the flexibility to take a breather with your infant.

86| Sail Away, Sail Away - To Europe

Going on a trip to Europe with baby once meant hopping on a long plane flight, booking a hotel, and trekking around with baby in a backpack. These days, the travel industry says cruising to Europe is gaining in popularity. We can see why. You have the option to take a shorter flight to the embarking port.

Enjoy a leisurely cruise across the Atlantic Ocean on a self-contained ship that feeds you, entertains you, and otherwise keeps you occupied with activities while you get ready to explore at different ports of call. If you live in Fort Lauderdale, you're in luck - a good number of ships depart from here to set sail on a European cruise. To give you an idea of some possible itineraries, we've listed a few cruises for the 2007 season.

If you've got quite a bit of time, Princess Cruises has a 17-day voyage departing in early May which takes you from Fort Lauderdale to stops at nine ports of call. You'll first stop off at Azores Islands. From there stop at Lisbon, Portugal, in Vigo, Spain, in Paris, France, in London, England, in Brussels, Belgium, in Rotterdam, Netherlands, in Oslo, Norway, and finish the cruise in Copenhagen, Denmark.

If you're looking for a shorter cruise, try one with a more specific itinerary and fly directly to a port of call in Europe. Carnival Cruises will take you on a 12-day cruise from Rome, Italy. From there stop in Naples, Italy, in Rhodes, Greece, in Izmir, Turkey, in Istanbul, Turkey, in Athens, Greece, in Katakolon, Greece, in Livorno, Italy, and then return to Rome, Italy.

If you want something a little more upscale, go with Cunard Cruises. You can go on a cruise as long as 22 days or for as brief as four days. For summer 2007, you can visit Europe with a sampler cruise and begin your journey in Southhampton, England. From there make a pit-stop in Hamburg, Germany before you make the two-day trip back to Southhampton.

87| Smooth Sailing On A Cruise With Baby

Like any other adventure with an infant in tow, sailing the high seas requires a bit of planning and open-mind to make the trip go smoothly. For those who are a bit wary of falling on their sea legs, read our guide to cruising with baby.

- Choose your destination wisely. Don't pick a cruise to Antarctica with baby just because you've been dying to go. Consider a warm weather or tropical location like the Caribbean or Hawaii. Then, book with a family-friendly cruise line. The last thing you want to do is end up on the party cruise with a group of spring breakers when you're trying to settle into a family vacation.

- When you book, find out what amenities your room will have. Many cruise cabins come with mini fridges so you can store all of baby's food and milk. Also inquire about portable cribs. Your cruise line should be able to supply you with one.

- A suite on the ship will create a nice sleep environment for baby and at the same time allow you plenty of space to enjoy some down time. Of course, a suite will cost you more. But there are some lines that have decent size cabins with families in mind. Disney Cruises have generous sized cabins if you're contemplating a cruise to the Bahamas or Caribbean. Book a room too small and you'll end up having to remove some furniture to accommodate a crib.

- Use the babysitting services or arrange to switch off with your spouse, a friend, or family member. You'll need some time to enjoy the on-board activities, ports of call, and shore excursions.

- Bring a stroller and take a walk around on deck. It's a great way to get some fresh air, enjoy the scenery, and relax. If your infant will take a nap, bring a book or magazine so you can relax, too.

- On a cruise, like any trip, remember to be flexible. Though booking every shore excursion you can squeeze in might work for singles and childless parents, with baby in tow you should plan your excursions carefully.

88| Your Cruise Upgrade Wishlist

If you're not against spending a little extra cash, there are some upgrades you can ask for when you book a cruise with baby. The least expensive rooms are inside cabins with no view. Next up in price are outside cabins on a cruise ship. It's always nice to have a view, but if you're going to splurge, we'd go for a room with a view – and some fresh air. Cabins with decks let you go outside and enjoy the view. Choose one of these if you're sailing on a scenic cruise. Also consider a suite or mini-suite. It's big enough to allow you space to hang out in the cabin, without disturbing your little one's nap.

So how much does it all cost? It'll vary based on factors including the time of year you travel, which cruise line you choose, and your destination. But to give you an idea of just how much you'll pay for cabin upgrades, here's a sample price list for 2007.

For a 7-day round trip cruise on Norwegian in April:
Inside Cabin - $599
Oceanview – $699
Balcony – $1049
Suite - $1249

Helpful Hint: Not all cruise lines and ships are built alike. Compare different cruise lines to see which ship has the kind of cabin you're interested in and the itinerary you want. For instance, the Emerald Princess of Princess Cruises has a suite and a mini-suite. The Norwegian Star of Norwegian Cruises only has a suite option.

Outdoor Travel with Babies

89| Feeding Baby At The Campsite

Going camping with an infant means you'll have to make do without a lot of conveniences that you have at home, or even a hotel. You'll have to be a little more creative in planning for the basics, like food and drink, for your little one. Lest you end up at the campsite struggling to mix formula with bottled water and attempting to warm it up over the fire pit, we've compiled a few handy tidbits that might make feeding your baby easier.

- If your baby is on formula, get the ready-made liquid version. We promise, it's easier than powder and the extra cost will be worth it.

- Bring a portable bottle and food warmer that operates without electricity if you need to warm up baby's food.

- If you have a toddler, you can pack powdered milk as a non-perishable alternative. Also, if soymilk is an option for you, Silk Soymilk has boxed versions of their calcium enriched drinks that don't require refrigeration.

- If you're using a cooler, use a block of ice instead of cubes to keep the food cold. Blocks stay frozen longer and your food will keep longer.

- You can bring baby jar food with you, but we like packing baby food into one-ounce sized cube trays. You don't have to worry about glass jar breakage and the individual portions are completely self-contained. We like *Baby Cubes from One Step Ahead*. They seal up tightly and you can throw them all into a Ziploc bag for your trip.

90| Camping At A KOA

So what do you do if you still really want to have the camping experience, but you don't want to do away with all the comforts of home?

One way to experience the outdoors with your infant yet still have access to a lot of amenities is by going to a Kampgrounds of America (KOA) location. They have campsites throughout the United States and Canada. You can bring a tent if you prefer. But you also have the option to hook up an RV, or rent a cabin, lodge, or cottage.

KOA calls their lodges "Kabins." They're basic one to two room structures with windows, doors, and a porch. You bring your own sleeping bag, cooking equipment, gear, and you're all set. Lodges follow the same concept. But you also get the benefit of your own shower, toilet, and kitchen, as well as a separate bedroom. Spelled with a "k", the Kottages are souped-up versions of the basic cabin. Bathrooms and even kitchens come with some versions of KOA Kottages.

For those who truly cannot be apart from the World Wide Web, a number of KOA campsites offer Internet access. But if you can bear to tear yourself away from the computer screen, you'll also be pleased to know that you can find some sites with swimming pools and miniature golf as well.

91| The Camping Trip

If you're a family that craves the outdoors, a camping trip in a tent with your baby might just be what you're looking for. Camping - at least the kind in tents - tends to be a hit or miss vacation with families with infants. Some parents think it's a wonderful way to get acquainted with baby. Some parents find it especially challenging to watch over a mobile infant or toddler among the outdoors and camping gear. Still, if you're up for it, here are some things to keep in mind.

- Pick a campground that's as baby-friendly as possible. A flat site is better than one with a steep drop-off. Amenities like laundry facilities and running hot water aren't a necessity, but certainly make it easier when you're dealing with infant messes.

- Stock up on the essentials you need for baby, like diapers, wipes, milk or formula, and baby food. You generally need everything you would need at home, but in convenient packable containers.

- Bring lots of plastic containers for packing away food. Have a store of plastic bags for disposing dirty diapers and other throwaway items.

- Bring a structured backpack carrier like one by *Kelty* for your child, especially if you plan on taking hikes. Soft carriers like one made by *Ergo* are appropriate for younger babies on up to toddlers.

- Many tents use a tarp underneath for protection and waterproofing. Get an extra one and you can use it as a play area.

- Bring a bottle of hand sanitizer. It's portable and comes in handy for cleaning up after messes.

- If you have a toddler, going camping will take some adjusting. Do a practice run by setting up the tent at home and acquainting your little one to the environment.

- It's always a good idea to have a few portable toys on hand at the campsite to entertain your little one.

- Don't forget to pack sunscreen for baby and parents. Go with an SPF 30 and apply every 30 minutes if you can.

- If you're going to an area with a lot of mosquitoes, you can use up to 30% DEET on infants as least two months old. For those who are adverse to DEET, Tender Corporation makes a product called *Natrapel* which is DEET free; some parents swear by it.

92| Sun Safety In The Outdoors

Any trip to the outdoors means you'll be spending a fair amount of time in the sun. Keep in mind that an infant's skin is much more sensitive than an adult's and more prone to burning. So it's always a good idea to keep safety precautions in mind during your vacation. Read on to find out what safety measures you can take to keep your baby away from the sun's harmful rays.

- Cover your baby up in clothing that will protect him from the sun. This means wearing a hat and long pants and shirts. You can also dress your child up in clothing which blocks UV rays. *Coolibar* (www.coolibar.com) sells infant swimwear, sun rompers, and hats which block out 98 percent of the UV rays.

- To protect infant's eyes, get a pair of UV protective shades. *Baby Bandz* sells sunglasses custom made to wrap around an infant's face and stays put with an elastic band. Never get sunglasses that aren't UV protective. They're actually more damaging to your eyes because the darkened appearance causes your pupils to let in more UV light.

- Use sunblock with an SPF of 30, and reapply every 30 minutes if your infant is over six months of age. If your baby will be in the water, don't forget to use a waterproof sunblock. You should also do a spot test on your infant's skin first to make sure she doesn't have any reactions.

- Whenever possible, keep your baby in the shade, especially if baby is under six months of age. Under a tree, under a tent shelter, or in a backpack with a sunshade are good places to protect baby from the sun.

- Keep in mind that the sun's rays are strongest from 10 AM to 4PM. Both you and your baby should not be exposed to the sun's rays for prolonged periods of time without any sun protection.

93| The Beach Trip

Beach trips make ideal vacations for families with babies. If you're contemplating a beach trip with baby, we recommend renting a beach condo or beach house – you have all the amenities of home, but in an entirely new setting. Set up a beach tent shelter outside and read a book while baby takes a nap. Pack some groceries or buy them once you arrive in town and eat a picnic outdoors. Wondering where to go? Some of the most popular beach spots around the United States for families include beaches in California, Florida, or Texas.

California has its very own Catalina Island. You can get there by a ferry that runs every hour. The island is full of shops, restaurants, and water activities to explore. For a more outdoorsy alternative to a vacation rental, stay at Two Harbors and rent a tent cabin.

In Florida, try Amelia Island, just a 30-minute drive from Jacksonville International Airport. You can get there via bridge and choose from outdoor activities like hiking, bird watching, and biking. Or take a stroll around the historic town and venture into their shops and restaurants.

In Texas, a great spot for families is South Padre Island in Galveston. You'll likely want to avoid going during the Spring Break period, because it's a popular college party spot, but during the rest of the year it's great for families. Take baby with you on a day cruise in the summer and try to spot dolphins. Or go out to the sand to enjoy the sandcastle classes.

LifeTips.com > > Outdoor Travel with Babies

94| Hedging Your Bets With Travel Insurance

For those who really like to be prepared, you can protect yourself against total loss in a trip due to things like inclement weather, missing baggage, travel delays, and unforeseen family tragedies with travel insurance. We think you should purchase insurance on a case-by-case basis. Weekend trips out of town or even a week-long rental for a beach trip to a nearby city probably doesn't warrant travel insurance. Insurance can be a good idea if, for instance, you're booking an all-inclusive vacation to the Bahamas and you want to protect yourself against the possibility of a hurricane.

The cost of insurance varies according to the cost of the trip and the age of the travelers. According to Staci Blunt of *Family Friendly Travel*, travel insurance with a big travel package provider like Apple Vacations might run you just under $70 per person. As another option, you can get travel insurance through a private party. Access America provides travel insurance for everything from cruises to business trips.

Helpful Hint: Some credit card companies come with built-in travel insurance if you pay for your vacation through them. Check with your credit card company to find out just what you might and might not be covered for.

95| Weather Warnings For Travelers

Often, when it comes time to plan a vacation, we think of new sights, new experiences, and getting away from it all in a pleasant environment. We bet your vision of vacation time isn't that far off. But one thing travelers have to be wary about is dealing with inclement weather – especially if you're going to be indulging in outdoor travel. We've put together just a few of Mother Nature's fierce weather conditions that you might want to know about before you plan your trip to the outdoors.

Flash Floods – Flash floods just six inches deep can knock you down if the water is moving fast enough. At two feet, your car will float. If you encounter flood waters, the best thing to do is turn around and move to higher ground.

Hurricanes – Nothing can ruin a perfectly good tropical vacation like a hurricane. Hurricanes have winds that can sustain speeds of 74 miles an hour or more. Hurricane season typically begins in the beginning of June and lasts through the end of November. The good news is you have access to a warning system 24 hours before one is expected to hit.

Thunderstorms – Thunderstorms can produce a few unpleasantries like 100 mile per hour winds and hailstones. If you're going to a campground, it's always a good idea to check what notification systems are in place in the event of severe weather like a thunderstorm. Also, find out what shelter areas are available should threatening weather hit.

Tornadoes – Fast and furious, tornadoes whip through at winds of 250 miles per hour or more. They're most common east of the Rocky Mountains in the spring and summer. You'll also find them occurring in the South from March to May. Northern states may have tornadoes from late spring into summer.

Tsunamis – Earthquakes and volcanic eruptions can cause a massive crash of waves known as the Tsunami. As soon as you hear a tsunami warning, head to higher ground.

Helpful Hint: The National Oceanic and Atmospheric Administration (NOAA) is the source to go to for checking out severe weather conditions. Check out their Website at www.weather.gov.

96| How To Snag A Rental Car Upgrade

If you're planning on renting a car to get around while traveling, you probably want to know how you can get the most bang for your buck. After all, you don't want to spend all your funds on airfare and hotel accommodations, only to end up paying several hundred dollars for a rental car that can actually fit everyone, the car seat, and the luggage. You can get a free rental car upgrade just by knowing what to book and when. And you don't have to ask for it.

The best way to get a free upgrade is by booking the most popular model of car during the busiest time of the week. If you can deal with the economy class, book that one, since it's the cheapest and one of the first cars to be overbooked. Rental car companies will often give you a free upgrade if the car class you booked or the model you requested is not available. Here's the deal:

- Rental car companies tend to overbook the car reservations and economy models are the first to go.

- The most popular models of cars tend to be gone before the other models.

- If you're traveling to a major city, you can get an upgrade during the middle of the day and early in the week. That's when a lot of business travelers tend to have rental cars.

- If you're going to a resort destination, the best time to get an upgrade is on a Saturday afternoon, when most of their economy models are rented.

97| Stay Sane On A Road Trip

If you have an infant who travels exceptionally well in the car, be thankful for your blessings. For parents who dread the thought of hitting the road with baby, here is a list of things you can do to stay sane on the drive.

1. Make a pack list and have everything ready a few days before your road trip.

2. The night before you leave, pack absolutely everything non-perishable into the car. Food, milk, and other items should all be ready in their containers so you can just grab and go when you're ready.

3. Pack the necessities in a separate, easily accessible bag – like your diaper bag. Diapers, diaper cream, wipes, milk or formula, snacks, disposable bibs, plastic bags for trash, and utensils should all be within easy reach. A small cooler with ice also helps for storing perishables.

4. Don't forget a change of clothes in case of spills and mishaps. Bring one for baby and one for you.

5. Plan to leave so that baby will fall asleep during her typical naptime. Or try leaving in the early evening if your little one will sleep through a good portion of the night. The longer your infant sleeps in a car during a road trip, the better. However, don't wait so long to leave! You don't want your infant tired and cranky when you're about to get in the car.

6. If you can spare one parent or adult, have that person sit in the back to attend to the needs of baby.

7. If you're driving during the day, make appropriate rest stops for baby for feedings, stretching out, and enjoying the view.

8. Have toys and music on hand to soothe and entertain baby. You know what calms her best, so don't forget to pack what will keep her occupied and happy. When all else fails, singing works quite nicely with a lot of infants.

98| Take A Road Trip With A Tent Trailer

Car trips are one way to get to your destination, but if you have an infant who truly does well on a drive, consider taking a tent trailer on a road trip. You get the benefit of towing conveniences like a sink, toilet, and shower while you drive to your destination. A tent trailer is a great alternative for parents who want to hit the outdoors, but don't want to rough it in a tent – especially with a baby. For those who aren't familiar, a tent trailer, also known as a camping trailer, is a cross between a tent and a recreational vehicle. Most mid-sized vehicles can tow a tent trailer. However, this depends on the model of car and the size of the tent trailer. They may be as simple as a 12-foot long cabin which provides a place to eat, sleep, cook, and store your food. Or they may be 22-foot long cabins that provide multiple sleeping areas, a sink, kitchen, restroom, and a place to shower.

Helpful Hint: You can find some entry tent trailer models with all the basics that start at $4,500. But if you don't want to spend that much, you can probably find a used one for under $1,000. If you're going on a one-week trip and you want to rent a tent trailer, you have that option, too. You might spend anywhere from $350 to $600 for a week's rental.

99| Five Rules For Visiting Friends And Family

If Grandma and Grandpa are 300 miles away, or if your best friend lives in another time zone, it's possible you'll be called out for a visit. If that's the case, we've got some ideas that will make your journey and stay to go as smooth as possible.

1. Regardless of whether you're visiting with parents, in-laws, or a college buddy, make sure you communicate your plans and needs ahead of time. Though it is convenient to stay with loved ones, it's easy to let a lot of details fall by the wayside. Here are the essentials: accommodations, childproofing, childcare, house rules, and itinerary.

2. When in doubt of what you need to bring for baby, think of your packing needs this way – food, clothing, shelter, sleep, and poop. Think about how baby will eat, what she'll wear, where she'll be staying, how she'll sleep, and how you'll handle her diaper changes. It's a lot, but necessary for baby.

3. If traveling by car, you'll need a car seat. If traveling by plane, you'll need a car seat or child approved harness safety device for the plane. Don't forget to assess whether you need a stroller or baby carrier as well.

4. You don't have to pack up your entire house when traveling to visit your friends or family. You'll be much less stressed with less to carry and your hosts will appreciate less clutter. If you can buy an extra case of diapers when you get there, do so. If you can borrow a stroller instead of bringing your own, do so.

5. Even staying with your own parents requires a certain level of appreciation. Though grandparents are more than anxious to spend time with their grandchildren, having an infant or toddler around can be tiring. Plan to have some time where everyone will have a break if you're going on an extended stay. Pitch in and help out with chores and groceries where you can.

100| Railway Travel Basics

Once you've decided that train travel is your vacation of choice with your infant, you'll need to start thinking about the logistics. With train travel, you do have trade-offs to traveling by car. You don't have the flexibility of leaving, stopping, and going as you would if you were driving your own vehicle. However, you have the freedom of spending your time observing the landscape and exploring the train with your infant.

Here are some railway travel basics you'll need to consider when you're going with baby:

- The fare for train travel can be relatively affordable if you're doing a short railway trip and traveling coach. Kids under 2 share an adult seat and don't pay a fare.

- If you're going on an extended trip, you'll likely want to book your own sleeper accommodations on the train. With Amtrak, this can range from the smaller roomette with seats that convert into a bed to a family bedroom, which converts to sleep two adults and two children. The caveat to booking sleep arrangements is that the fares are much pricier.

- Book your tickets and accommodations early for extended travel. You probably don't want to be stuck with the entire family sleeping a few nights in coach seating – especially with an infant.

- Find out what amenities will be on your train. Amtrak may have meal services available, depending on the route and length of your trip. Most long distance routes have a dining car that serves hot meals and may require reservations. Some routes also have informal dining like a snack bar.

- As far as luggage is concerned, you do have a two-piece limit per person. You can also check an additional three pieces of luggage if you really need to bring that much with you. As you would expect, it's advisable to pack as light as possible.

- You do need to bring a portable crib for baby. Remember train accommodations are tight and you won't be able to fit much of anything in your room. For infants, take a look at the *Peapod Travel Bed* by Kidco ($50). It folds into a bag for travel and pops open for sleeptime.

- Snacks, beverages, formula, diapers, and other essentials are important as well, since you won't be able to make a stop at a store and you don't want to be without while you're on the train. Though meals and snacks may be available, don't assume they'll have what you need or want to feed baby.

- We also suggest you bring a baby carrier for younger infants, since you'll want to have your hands free while moving about.

101| U.S. Train Travel

The train trip isn't what immediately comes to mind when families think about planning a trip for baby. Still, trains are a great alternative to traveling by car if you just want to travel by rail with baby. You won't have to worry about driving, you can have meals on the train, the view is scenic for you and baby, and some trains have on board entertainment. If you're considering traveling by railway in the U.S. with your infant, you'll most likely be traveling via Amtrak.

Amtrak has a network of trains that travel throughout the country. You can plan a vacation package with them which includes a combination of hotel accommodations, car rental, and sightseeing. You have a wide variety of Amtrak train trip itineraries to select from. Take a short train ride that lasts two and a half hours from Los Angeles to San Diego. Or take a day and a half to ride up the California coast from Los Angeles to Seattle. You can also venture on a two-day trip across the Rocky Mountains from Emeryville in the West Coast to Chicago by the Great Lakes. In the Northeast, take a train trip from New York to Niagara Falls on a full day's ride.

Want more ideas? Amtrak posts their train schedules and travel times on their Website at www.amtrak.com.

Acknowledgements

I'd like to express my thanks to all the baby travel savvy parents who shared with me their own knowledge and experiences.

Staci Blunt, CTC, CTP
Owner
Family-Friendly Vacations
2234 S. Estrella
Mesa, AZ 85202
Tel. 480-664-8918 or 800-664-8918
www.family-friendlyvacations.com

Jackie Chang

Miranda Chin
Travel Consultant
Hawaii & Beyond
415-381-6477

Alan Fields, Co-Author of Baby Bargains
www.BabyBargains.com

Natalie Lorenzi

Strollerqueen
www.strollerqueen.com

And Kip Wilson

More Titles in the LifeTips Book Series

101 Health Insurance Tips
by Michelle Katz

101 Sports Apparel Tips
by Heidi Splete

101 Vacation RentalsTips
by Dawn Anderson-Meier

101 Plus-Size Wedding Attire Tips
by Lynda Moultry

101 Student Loan Tips
by Lynne Christen

Printed in the United States
115030LV00001B/2/A